CLOUDS AND SUNSHINE

CLOUDS AND SUNSHINE

Ray Powell

ATHENA PRESS
LONDON

CLOUDS AND SUNSHINE
Copyright © Ray Powell 2007

All Rights Reserved

No part of this book may be reproduced in any form
by photocopying or by any electronic or mechanical means,
including information storage or retrieval systems,
without permission in writing from both the copyright
owner and the publisher of this book.

ISBN 10-digit: 1 84748 028 4
ISBN 13-digit: 978 1 84748 028 6

First Published 2007 by
ATHENA PRESS
Queen's House, 2 Holly Road
Twickenham TW1 4EG
United Kingdom

Printed for Athena Press

For my family

This is for all of you, for this is your heritage. I have tried to paint a picture, not only of my early years, but of what I think was a unique time in our social history.

It is not only a record of those times but also an insight into the events that shaped the lives of Joan and me and indirectly you.

I hope you enjoy and treasure it, I hope also that it will be of interest to future generations.

My family
Photograph by J Smith

Ray Powell
Photograph by Mandy Tully

Acknowledgements

I must thank Joan (as always) for her support, encouragement and endless hours of proofreading and correcting what I call my 'grammar'. She has read this so often I am sure she could recite it by heart if I ever lost the copy. It is Joan who has made this readable, and I owe her an enormous debt for her help.

If this book has any literary merit it is due in no small measure to my great friend, Brian Davidson (*El Prof*), who has given me a one-man writing course. He also has read and reread every line, I shall always be grateful for his unstinting help.

Fuengirola, January 2004

Contents

The Railway	11
Monmouth	17
Villages and Hamlets	30
Wyeswood	33
Catbrook	37
School Days	43
War	49
Whitelye	51
The War Years	52
The Dawn of Hope	64
Last Days at Whitelye	73
The Aftermath	76
Swansea and After	82
The Fifties	85
Wyeswood – The Final Chapter	96
Epilogue: Sixty Years Later	101
Appendix: My Parents	107

The Railway

A child wakes screaming in the night. In his nightmare he sees a great black steaming monster coming out of a tunnel towards him. Quickly his mother lifts him out of his cot and comforts him. The child was me. The monster was a railway engine coming out of the tunnel, over the Wye Bridge into Tintern Station.

Tintern Station and the Wye Valley Line were to be a thread running through my life from my babyhood to my marriage in 1952. It was from here that my father sent his chicks and eggs all over the country. It was from here that my brothers went to, and returned from, the war. It was our saviour when we were snowed in during the record winter of 1947. My last trip ever from Tintern was with my bride in 1952 and our return a week later. No one will ever make that lovely journey through the Wye Valley again. From Chepstow to Ross, the halts and stations are a litany of some of the most beautiful and historic towns and villages of Britain.

Tintern, Brockweir, Llandogo... and the curiously named St Briavels Junction. Here there was no junction, and anyone alighting would have a shock on finding that St Briavels was two miles away, mostly uphill! There is a hamlet here called Bigsweir, chiefly noteworthy for being the tidal limit of the River Wye. On then to Redbrook, which received the coal from the Forest of Dean and the steel from the Redbrook Tinplate Works. Next stop was Monmouth: the last county town to have a railway service and the first to lose it!

Out of Monmouth Mayhill Station, the line followed not only the river but also Offa's Dyke. The river here not only separates Monmouth from Gloucester but also Wales and England. This is truly Marcher country now, as the line passes Goodrich, Symonds Yat and finally reaches Ross-on-Wye.

This then was the locality in which I grew up. It's not where I was born, as that event occurred some ten weeks before my family moved to Wyeswood, but it is where I always think of as my native land. Tintern was a large sprawling village, with many happy memories for me.

The main street runs parallel to the river and ends at the famous Tintern Abbey so extolled by the poet Wordsworth. The guidebooks tell us about it being a Cistercian abbey, but all seem to miss the most vital events.

The most notable feature is the high circular window that provides a perfect frame for the September full moon (the harvest moon). At one time coach loads of people came to view this spectacular event until it got out of hand and the police stopped it.

It was the monks of Tintern Abbey who were the first to make an alloy of zinc and copper to make the metal we know as brass, thus laying the foundation of huge industries and making possible all the hygiene and toilet facilities we have today. Some years ago the National Brassfounders Association installed a plaque there to commemorate this great achievement.

The abbey now stands gaunt and roofless. Originally the roof was made of lead but Henry VIII stole it for his own personal needs, which proves that there is nothing new in today's nefarious activities.

Forming a T with the main street, the road moves through the oldest part of the village to the area known as 'Pont-y-Saeson' meaning 'Saxon Bridge' – so called from a battle between the Celts and Saxons. I shall always have a soft spot for this area, as here lived my first real love.

On this road was the Cherry Tree inn, the meeting place of the Tintern Abbey Motorcycle Club, for about five years from 1948 to 1953. These clubs were great fun for anyone interested in motorcycling. Our meeting place was only coincidental; the club's aim was to promote responsible riding, and to encourage those interested in the sport. This was controlled by the ACU (Autocycling Union) who imposed strict standards of safety on all sporting events; thankfully this control did not extend to the rest of our activities.

The club gave us a great change from the boring post-war period. At long, long last we were getting free of the rationing and shortages that had held us back for so long. It was not until 1950 that petrol rationing was finally abolished, and our sport could really take off again and the 'open road' was once more really open.

Turning back east the road takes us back through the village and past the pub known now as the Moon and Sixpence. In our day it was the Mason's Arms kept by a widower and his two daughters, with whom my friend Frank and I became friendly. Sadly all this came to an end on VJ night when, after running out of beer, the landlord went out with friends. The car stopped suddenly and he went out through the sunshine roof and was killed.

Next to the pub there was a seat provided by the council. Whether the seat was for visitors or for couples I don't know, but it could tell a few tales for sure.

Travelling back East past Tintern Parva Farm... In my day a Mr Robinson owned this. There was an occasion one evening during the war when he crossed the road for a five-minute job of letting his cows out. Unfortunately, just as he crossed the road, an American army convoy came through. Two hours later a very hungry Mr Robinson was able to return home.

Next village on the way is Brockweir. I got to know this village in my teens, partly because of it being in England and partly because of the very good dances that they had there. Being in England meant that the pubs were open on Sunday nights. Owing to the beer shortage they only opened for two hours. If we were a little late we could see, from the hill above, the crowd outside. As soon as the doors opened the crowd disappeared like water down a plughole. We had to be there early because the landlord would run out of glasses. If we felt like going to the other pub we would (very naughtily) take our glasses with us.

As the road goes on towards Llandogo, the scenery changes. On the Gloucester side the woods recede for a while. On the Monmouth side wooded hills appear which lead us to Llandogo, surely the prettiest village on the Wye.

Llandogo was a sleepy sort of place and has no violent history that I know of. The name, I have been told, comes from its association with Llandoger Trow near Bristol, from where the trows (a sort of shallow boat) made their way with goods from Bristol docks to the Wye Valley until the railway came. I believe that the Sloop Inn gets its name from this trade.

I had many happy times here, as this was the nearest village with a pub, and in time I came to make quite a few friends in the village. It was also the nearest stopping point for train and bus. During the war the trees above the valley were felled, giving us a marvellous view of the river, railway line and road. One winter's morning I came down to catch a bus just after a snowfall. After over fifty years and travel in many countries, the image of the village covered in virgin snow remains one of the most beautiful sights I have ever seen.

Of the families there, I particularly remember the Browns from the Eddis Tea Gardens, and the Morgans who kept the farm. Both families were roughly the same age as us. I recall especially going to a dance at St Briavels with them in 1944. Victor Morgan was serving in the RAF as an Air Gunner. He had completed twenty-eight ops and was looking forward to a rest after he had completed another two. Sadly, on the thirtieth op his Lancaster was shot down over Germany with the loss of all the crew.

At the top of the village was the Lion Inn (now sadly no more) kept by Charlie Parker. He was a great character, and the place was really our local, being only a mile from Wyeswood. We had many happy times there; I must have been a good customer as I was allowed to join the select band of Sunday morning backdoor clients. The qualification for membership was to be able to consume four pints in about an hour. Charlie was not going to risk his licence for someone standing around drinking a solitary half-pint.

Just down from the Lion was the doctor's surgery, a lovely spot at the bottom of the Cleddon Waterfall. It was only open on Thursday afternoons, so for anything urgent one had to travel to St Briavels to Dr Nanda's surgery. Not that he officiated at the surgery; he was far too grand for that. The medical needs of the area, comprising – Tintern, Catbrook, Trelech, Llandogo and all the houses, farms and hamlets – were provided by his assistant, who in addition to home visits held surgeries in all the villages. He was a small man who literally bounced around the roads in a Morris Eight car. He had no time to stand on ceremony. When I was ill with rheumatic fever, more than once he had entered the house, examined me, and was on his way out before my mother knew he was there.

Before leaving Llandogo I must go back to the river again. Here, in early spring, the baby eels or elvers, having survived their journey from the Saragossa Sea, would move up the river with the tide in great clumps. Elvers pressed into cakes like cheeses were considered a great delicacy and made good prices. Llandogo was a prime site for catching them, as the river was very accessible, and also the last place to catch them, as they were not edible in the non-tidal part of the river.

We are still following the 'three Rs' here, but the road slips over to the other side of the river at Bigsweir Bridge, and faithfully follows the river to Redbrook village.

For some reason Redbrook was divided between Gloucester and Monmouth; and, it boasted four pubs when I knew it. Of these, two were on one side and two on the other. While the Monmouth landlords may not have been happy, it did provide another Sunday drinking option for the thirsty folk of Monmouth.

I only availed myself of this option once. It was a lovely June morning, and as I was early for my first date with Joan (my future wife) I stopped for a drink on the way. Sitting out on the pub lawn looking out at the river was very pleasant. The first pint went down rather quickly so I had another. I enjoyed that so much that I had another (as one does). By the time I had drunk that one, time had gone rather more quickly than I realised, so I had a bit of fast driving to do to make the date. It was only due to the milk lorry driver chatting up Joan that I made it before she gave up on me. The rest, as they say, is history.

Here at Redbrook, the railway came back over the river and the road before going on to Wyesham and Monmouth (Mayhill). After Mayhill the line continued to Ross-on-Wye. The countryside changes here, because we have moved from the shadow of the Forest of Dean to the flatter, rich lands of Herefordshire – the land of red soil and white faces. The 'white faces' refer not to the people but the world-famous Hereford cattle. No animal, except possibly the Merino sheep of Spain, has contributed so much to human welfare. These animals were so hardy that they could exist in good or harsh conditions anywhere in the world. They and their descendants are to be found all over South America, the prairies of the USA and in Canada.

My family has many connections with this area. My great-, great-grandfather was born near here, and many descendants lived in Herefordshire. My father was born in the county. It was near here that I had the only holiday I ever had as a child, when I spent two weeks with my uncle at Weston-under-Penyard in that fateful August of 1939. I remember my mother almost in tears as we saw the headlines forecasting an imminent war as we went through Ross.

The 1821 census of Weston-under-Penyard records that: an 'increase of machinery and consequent idleness is supposed to have caused an increase of bastardy in the village'.

The line from Monmouth passed through a valley so beautiful that it inspired the poet Wordsworth to those immortal lines:

> O Sylvan Wye! Thou wanderer through the woods,
> How often has my spirit turned to thee!

I think that it is at Symonds Yat (yat=Old English for promontory) where the river describes an almost perfect horseshoe bend around the yat. If you stand on the top it is possible to see the river on both sides of the promontory.

Having had that brief look at Herefordshire, I will return to my beloved Monmouthshire, and its lovely county town of Monmouth.

Monmouth

A small boy watches wide-eyed as a soldier blows a fanfare on his bugle. A red-robed figure climbs out of a car and walks slowly into the Shire Hall. With him he takes centuries of history. What the boy is seeing is the last Assize Court ever to be held in Monmouth. For almost a thousand years this has been the seat of justice for Monmouthshire, and the ancient 'Archenfield'. The phrase 'being in the carts for Monmouth' was synonymous with summary trial, execution or transportation. It was in this court that the 'Chartist' rioters were dealt with. The boy is of course myself; the bugler is by coincidence a neighbour of ours, Wilson Morris, who is there as a member of the local Territorial unit, the 'Royal Monmouthshire Royal Engineers', the only regiment of the British Army to boast two 'Royals' in its title.

Before I go on with my memories of the town, a few notes on its location. Nestling in the valley just above the confluence of the rivers Wye and Monnow, to the east the road leads out of the county to Hereford, a city of bittersweet memories for Joan and myself, as this is where our first son was born, only to live for a day; a child whom we never held and I saw but once. He now sleeps the long sleep in the shade of Belmont Abbey. Later our son Tony was born there.

To the west the road runs back to Chepstow. To the south the Kymin Hill rises above the river. The Kymin is infamous for being the place where Lord Nelson used to take Lady Hamilton for a spot of illicit nooky, a practice that the local lads have been following ever since. To the north the road takes us to the villages where I grew up, of which more later.

No one writing of Monmouth could leave out a picture of the famous old Norman bridge. This is the only example of a fortified bridge in Britain. If any picture means Monmouth, this is it. Not only did it survive the town's turbulent past but its hardest knocks came during WWII. Being the only route through the town for very long vehicles, the American army tank transporters hit it with everything they had. Ten years later Wynn's Transport, carrying girders for the Trostre steelworks gave it the same treatment; but still the old bridge survived as it has done for a thousand years, and will probably survive for another thousand.

My first memory of the place that was to mean so much to me was travelling with my parents up Cinderhill Street. In those days there were houses lining both sides of the street. The Labour Exchange was in St Thomas's Square, and I remember now asking what the lines of men were doing in the street. It was of course Friday, and the men were queuing to get their dole money. Then it was up to the bridge leaving the Three Horseshoes inn on the left. This was to be the last inn in the town where my father was able to stable his horse. It was about 1954 when he had to stop; he was the last man to do this, and when he finished, centuries of tradition ceased and the motor had finally won. By strange coincidence my Uncle Sid, using the same trap, was the last man ten years later to take a pony and trap to Abergavenny.

Up through Monnow Street we reach the Beaufort Arms, where my father stabled his horse every Friday for a dozen years until the Army requisitioned the hotel in 1940. I remember him having a horse called 'Noble'; every time that he drove out of the courtyard the horse would rear up, scattering people far and wide. Once Noble had done this, he trotted off docilely down the street, leaving the frightened pedestrians to recover their wits.

While my father went about his business my mother went shopping. As there were seven of us my mother was a valuable, if careful, customer. George Mason's had a grocer's shop off Agincourt Square then. As soon as we entered, the manager called out, 'Chair for Mrs Powell.' Whereupon the shop boy duly produced a chair for Mum. When I say 'careful customer', that's what she was. In those days sugar was bagged in the shop; I've seen her make the girl undo the bag so she could inspect the sugar. Some shops had to get fifty 2lb bags out of a 100lb bag, and as some always got spilled the assistant was apt to make up the shortfall with a bit of sand. After the order was completed it was put into her shopping baskets to be delivered to the Beaufort Arms later.

After the shopping they would meet up at the produce market. This was held at the top of the town, but was another war casualty when it had to be moved to the Borough Arms, where Dad had to stable his horse. The market was where farmers and county folk sold eggs, butter, garden seedlings, jams and preserves in season, while others sold surplus garden produce. Women and the unemployed also gathered wild fruit to sell here and supplement their meagre incomes. One particular delicacy was whimberries, which ripened about June and were particularly prolific around the 'top of the hill', i.e. the Catbrook area. These were awful things to pick, but nevertheless there was great excitement in the first weeks when the price reached a shilling (5p) a pound – the result of probably a solid hour's tedious, back-breaking work.

I think that early childhood memories are like a spring day; as the clouds pass another memory appears. Perhaps I should start at the lower end of Monnow Street and move upwards. First we come to Marleen's café, started by a bus driver with his service gratuity and named after his daughter. I used to get a bit of stick from the Red & White bus company staff (the company was started by a WWI veteran with his gratuity) because of my different political views. In the 1951 election I could hardly eat my lunch for the ribaldry. However I had the last laugh as we very nearly won.

From Marleen's to another café, this time the Cosy. Colonel Harry Llewellyn, who gained great success showjumping with his horse 'Foxhunter', owned this. He later renamed the café the 'Foxhunter Café'. When I worked for Len Hunt, the girls there, especially Mollie, gave us many a 'freebie' coffee.

Past the bus station to the Vine Tree inn. Next door Jeff Davies opened a motorcycle business just after the war. Jeff was a first-class engineer who had worked as a racing mechanic, especially in the Isle of Man. His shop was a magnet for us motorcycle nuts, and from him I bought my first really good motorbike, a two-year-old BSA 250cc on which I travelled many happy miles. His mechanic was Billy Hamer from Skenfrith, again a good mechanic, who later set up his own business.

Further up, I recall the smell of leather from McEwen & Baynham's saddlery shop, where my father bought his horse harness. Next up was the Electricity Board, where I worked for a time in the early fifties. I remember in particular three workmates. The first of these was John Tunnicliffe, a Northerner who came to Monmouth in the late twenties when GEC took over the local electricity company. At that time Monmouth only had one main electricity supply, taken in at Redbrook. When the supply failed John had to jump on his bike and pedal furiously the three miles to Redbrook to restore the supply. Another whom I worked with was Vic White. He unfortunately had to take early medical retirement due to the ill-treatment he received when a Japanese prisoner of war.

Perhaps the most memorable of all was Tommy Edwards, one of the best workmates I ever had. Tommy had been brought up with his grandparents, as his father had been killed in Britain's worst pit disaster at Senghenydd (which killed 436 men) before he was born. Everyone in the town knew Tommy, and he was a familiar sight pushing his carrier bike laden with tools and meters. Tommy was always in such a hurry that he rarely had time to actually ride his bike, which was due not only to his workload but also his dalliance with a lady whose husband worked irregular shifts. Unfortunately for him, the lady wore a rather pungent perfume, and on many evenings I sprayed him with the fire extinguisher before sending him home!

Apart from his other qualities he was also a very kind man. One of his duties was to inspect the work of other companies before connecting to the mains. Many inspectors took delight in failing other people's work, but not Tom. I have known him to find the electrician to tell him to put things right, or to connect the supply but warn the offender to put things right. It is a tribute to the respect in which he was held that no one ever let him down. Every month he was given a list of customers who had not paid their electricity and had to be cut off. He was always given this list last thing at night. It was a job he always hated, and often he would spend two hours of his own time going around telling the people to pay next morning before he had to cut them off. Again he was rarely let down. During the war Tommy had served as aircrew in the RAF. All aircrew on leave were justly proud of the 'wings' they wore. Tommy was different, to save his relatives from worry he never told them he was on flying duties, and before going on leave he would remove his wings from his tunic. After all this he died from slipping on ice and striking his head on the pavement.

The street takes me up past the long gone Taylor & Jones, ironmongers, agricultural machinery and radios! (My brother Ted worked there for six months before joining up; it was to be the last civilian job he would ever have.) To Agincourt Square, in the top corner of which was Woolworth's. What an Aladdin's cave that was to a young child in those days – and nothing over sixpence! Mum often took us there to warm up after the cold drive in the trap. In the other corner of the square was that horror of horrors – Timms the dentist – and it was some small satisfaction that this was about the only place in Monmouth to be hit by a bomb in the war.

Close by there was a newsagent's kept by the Howes family. During the war they posted the daily paper to us; it was never late. Later, in about 1948/49, I became friendly with the son, Donald, both being members of the Young Conservatives. He had won the Military Cross for bravery at the Rhine Crossing in 1945. He was particularly kind to me on one occasion. We had entered a team for a public speaking contest. I was picked to speak for three minutes. During one practice session he told me not to worry about my speech hesitation, saying, 'It's rather attractive and makes people listen.' Great fellow that he was, I don't think he could realise what those words meant to me. After being mocked and ridiculed about my speech, and the butt of many a joke, these were the first encouraging words anyone had ever said to me on the subject.

Out of the far corner of the Square is Church Street, at the end of which was the Gaumont British cinema, apart from pubs the only entertainment open to us during the war. Up to 1939 the bus company ran a bus to the Catbrook area for cinema-goers, which meant that the bus could not leave until the last picture was over and the last bag of fish and chips purchased. What pleasures we had here. With my friends Frank and Conk we bunked off school to see *The Great Dictator*, and as the film took the rise out of Hitler and Mussolini this was almost a patriotic duty. Later we fell for Margaret Lockwood, stared at Betty Grable's legs and watched the war films like *F for Freddy*. As we grew up our pleasures were not solely confined to the films, of course.

Turning sharp right here takes one into St Mary Street. Down here was Little's, the butchers, where I remember standing amazed at the sight of the sausages being made. Further down was a greengrocer's shop. No disrespect to the owner, but this represented a couple of examples of the hypocrisy of the forties and fifties. For some reason known only to the unions this was the only shop in Monmouth allowed to sell Sunday newspapers. The owner's other sideline was to operate a strictly illegal betting shop. Everyone knew of it but the police very sensibly ignored what was going on.

On the left side is the church which gives the street its name, the church where Joan and I were married, as were her parents some twenty-five years previously, and where our daughter, Wendy, was christened.

Turning right at the lower end takes me past the Grammar School where I believe the medieval poet, Geoffrey of Monmouth, worked. Before I bear right into Glendower Street I must mention the building on the left. As a small child I remember the sign 'PPP' that I was told stood for 'Powell Practical Printers'. Later I was to become friends with the son, Tony, without doubt one of the best friends I have ever had. A motor fitter by trade, when I first knew him he was employed as a patrolman by the AA. Driving several times a day between Monmouth and Abergavenny, he covered some 60,000 miles a year in all weathers. For this task he was equipped with a BSA motorcycle and sidecar full of all his tools etc. His opposite number working for the RAC was provided with a similar outfit but using a Norton motorcycle. When an opportunity occurred, they would relieve the boredom by having a race on the Raglan road.

I think the roads in Monmouth are different now. At that time one could turn back right to return to Agincourt Square, which brings me to the Agincourt Hotel. We had many a happy evening here, and varied was the crowd. One of these characters was 'Tex'. Tex had two hobbies: one was drinking a mixture of

Guinness and cider, the other hobby was playing the drums – and what better way of finishing the evening after drinking six pints of his favourite tipple than to go home and have a drum session! Sadly for Tex, neither his parents nor the neighbours appreciated a midnight serenade, thus putting a block on his musical career.

Passing through the square and turning left brought one to the establishment of KP Hall & Son, ladies' outfitters, haberdashery and house furnishings. Like many such places, the original KP Hall had long gone from the scene. In the late forties/fifties I became very friendly with the son, Colin, known to all as 'Jeep'. To say that Jeep was a character is a gross understatement. He was a rogue, cad, drinker, ladies' man and a bloody good mate. I met him first through the motorcycle club (Tintern Abbey MCC). I forget what bike he had at first, but he also possessed an ancient Riley 'Hornet'. When he later acquired a BSA Gold Star he persuaded his father that it would be a good idea to convert the Riley to carry rolls of lino and carpet. The fact that this modification made the car suitable for taking the bike to races was a pure coincidence, of course.

Jeep's father was a pillar of the local establishment. A local magistrate, he was also a long-suffering man who occasionally lost his patience with his son. They would fall out and Jeep had to take up temporary lodgings elsewhere until things cooled down. Mr Hall was one of the first persons to buy one the latest Austin A40 cars. As he wasn't a driver, it was his son who had to collect the car from the dealers, and as there was no garage at the house the car was kept in a lock-up some distance away.

On taking delivery, Jeep had the foresight to stop at the ironmonger's to acquire a duplicate set of both keys, thus enabling him and his friends to travel far and wide while Mr Hall sat at home in blissful ignorance.

Jeep was always thinking of ways to make money and ride bikes. One of which was to give up work and spend the summer scrambling on the continent. We did however spend a weekend in Brecon for the Eppynt races. Every May just before the Isle of Man TT there was road racing on this wonderful mountain circuit at Sennybridge. Jeep was having his first competitive race in the 'Clubman's' event. I went with him as his racing mechanic. My protestations that I was no mechanic were brushed aside, as the mechanic's badge was solely to get me into the riders' beer tent. In his event, Jeep came nowhere but we had a memorable time watching the racing and mixing with the big boys. Amongst these was the great AJS rider, Les Graham. Already famous before the war, in which he won the DFC as a fighter pilot, this was to be his last finish as he was killed two weeks later practicing for the TT.

The last story I have of this character concerns our wedding. Being somewhat late in leaving the reception we missed the train at Monmouth station. The stationmaster agreed to arrange for the train to wait for us at Tintern. Jeep stepped into the breech by offering to drive us, in the faithful A40 of course. Tony Powell, Den Morgan and Alma came along on a very memorable journey down the Wye Valley; memorable because he drove so fast we had to wait some time for the train to catch up with us! So on the greatest day of my life I returned to the place that had played so great a part in my and my family's life.

Continuing down Monnow Street brings me to the Butcher's Arms. This was kept by a Mr and Mrs Fred Preece. Fred was an archetypal publican. Weighing some twenty stone, he nevertheless lived in awe of Mrs Preece. I believe she restricted his smoking habit, as he was wont to cadge a fag from his customers. Leaning across the bar one evening to get a light for one of these fags he cracked a couple of ribs. Great hilarity was had by his regulars in guessing how many yards of plaster were used to strap him up. When I was working for the Electricity Board we would go over for a couple of half-pints after work. I got to know them quite well, so naturally this was where Joan and I went for our wedding reception. As Joan's mum had died some years previously, Joan had to make all the arrangements. Mrs Preece could not have been more kind and helpful, and it was due to her that it all went smoothly.

Lower down the street was Len Hunt's. In his early days he had been a successful racing cyclist, so naturally when he went into business in 1916 he opened a cycle shop. This must have been a low-key affair as he was still serving as a dispatch rider on the Western Front. Many years later, as I was going on a 200-mile rally his comment was, 'That's nothing! I've done that without lights under shellfire.' While the 200 miles may have been an exaggeration the rest certainly wasn't, and he had a bravery award to prove it. He was still dealing mainly in cycles when I first knew him, and most of the locals bought their cycles from him (mostly second-hand). My first cycles came from him and anyone cycling in from the country was able to leave their cycles with him while they went about their pleasures or business.

In the late thirties Len, with his son – also called Len – branched out into radio and public address work, and also had a couple of petrol pumps. It was during the war that the business really took off, since people now had some money and everything was in short supply, so a circular barter system developed. Petrol was of course severely rationed; however, some customers would get extra fuel for favours, usually farm produce. This resulted in a shortage of petrol coupons. To remedy this, Len took to adding a little TVO (Tractor Vaporising Oil, a sort of paraffin for farm tractors which was not rationed) to the petrol. This was highly illegal, of course, and would have resulted in a prison sentence if he had been caught; but as the local police depended on him to augment their rations with butter, eggs or other black market goods, this was not a worry for him.

I don't think he was basically a crook, but things got so out of hand that he found himself on a steadily descending spiral. After the war, when the government brought out red petrol for commercial vehicles, this proved ideal for the taxis Len was running. Again, this was no problem, as he was always told when a police check was due, which enabled him to empty the car tanks ready for dipping. It was undoubtedly a fact that those who indulged in these practices were those who had no member of their family serving in the forces. Some of his regular customers were farmers who got a cushy job with the War Ag (War Agricultural Executive Committee), thus allowing their sons to carry on working the farm. This exempted them from military service – and this at time when thousands of merchant seamen were dying bringing vital supplies to the UK.

I worked for Len for a time as a radio mechanic. Like so many, he believed in post-war prices but pre-war wages so I didn't stay long.

Next door to Len Hunt's was Roy Wilding's hairdressing

salon. Roy was known to all and sundry as 'Larrup'; Joan thought that was his real name and used to call him Mr Larrup. He was another ex-serviceman who started his business on his war gratuity. His one failing was his love of boxing. If a waiting customer started an argument on this sport, woe betide anyone who was in the chair, as he was liable revert to his army days and give one a very short 'short back and sides'.

At the bottom of the street you turn sharp left through the livestock markets to Chippenham Meadow. Here on the first Monday of May is held the 'Mop Fair'. Originally these were hiring fairs where farm labourers hired themselves out for the following year. It was also the occasion when they celebrated getting their wages. Many felt the day well spent if they got a job, a good skinful and possibly a fight into the bargain. My father has told me that even in the early twentieth century it was a place for having teeth extracted. Apart from these 'delights' it was full of stalls and cheapjacks. In my time it was mostly a funfair, with sweet stalls and the like. My memory of it is a bit hazy, as most of it, except the funfair, disappeared during the war.

Back now to Monnow Street for the last time, back over the old bridge and left into Cinderhill Street. From here it was a short distance to Troy Station, and here we leave the town behind and head into the country.

Shakespeare wrote in *Henry V*:

'There are many good men born in Monmouth
    Where the Monnow meets the Wye.'

I could not agree more. I am proud to have lived, worked and been part of it. My thanks go to Monmouth and all those who helped to make my time there so enjoyable and memorable.

Monmouth's most famous son, Henry V, was born in Monmouth Castle; from this area he recruited his famous archers the 'Bowmen of Gwent', who struck fear into the French at Crécy and Agincourt. The French hated them so much that they amputated the first and second fingers of any prisoners, as these two fingers were essential to the operation of the crossbow. It was this action that gave rise to the derisory two-fingered salute common today.

Tintern's ruined abbey. Harvest Moon at top.
Photograph from Castle of Wales website www.castlewales.com.

Monmouth's two most famous sons.

The other famous son is of course Charlie Rolls. Son of a local peer, he is best known for his association with Henry Royce, and of course the Rolls-Royce motor-car. He should be remembered for his work and courage as a pioneer aviator. Only Blériot beat him to being the first man to fly the English Channel, but he was the first to make a round trip across the channel. He was tragically killed in a flying accident in 1911.

Villages and Hamlets

As you leave Monmouth, the old A40 road is followed for a short time crossing the River Trothy on your way. Shortly after leaving the A40, bear left to take the Trelech/Chepstow road. Soon the road goes sharply upwards as Lydart Hill is reached. As a child, this was frightening for me, as Dad's horse would often slip on the road. Over the years I got to know almost every stone on the way. I have travelled it by foot, horse, cycle, motorcycle, car and anything else that moved. From this hill I could see over the country as far the Sugar Loaf Mountain. Normally a beautiful vista it was almost eerie at night during the war as the whole country was in total darkness, something not experienced since the Middle Ages.

Travelling now over the hill (always a relief) past the oddly named Gockett Inn is the turn for Whitebrook, the Narth and Pen-y-fan. It was at a farm near here that my brother suffered his fatal accident. There are now only a few scattered houses and farms until Trelech is reached.

This is a rather small place now with no industry of any sort and, I think, only one shop. In its heyday it was quite an important place. At the end of the eighteenth century it was bigger than Cardiff and was known as Trelech Town. The name is taken from three ancient standing stones or cromlechs.

The village played a vital role in my family's story. Stan, Bill and I were confirmed in the church. My brothers were choirboys there; this was quite an achievement, considering that the whole family was incapable of singing a single note in tune. My parents and brother Stan are buried there. In the church hall opposite I met my future wife. My brother Bill lived and had a dairy business at the bottom of the village for thirty years.

On the right-hand side is Court Farm, the only place in Trelech to be hit by a bomb during the war. By some mischance the bomb missed all the open fields and landed smack in the middle of the barn.

The road forks here, right to Llanishen and Chepstow, centre to Catbrook, and left to Cleddon and Llandogo. Adjacent to the left fork was a blacksmith's forge. The owner, one Victor Crum, died in 1940. With his death ended centuries of iron working in the village, the iron being mined and smelted in the nearby Forest of Dean.

Victor Crum and his wife had two sons. The elder son served in the Metropolitan Police before the war. In 1940 he joined the Fleet Air Arm but sadly disappeared on a training flight in the USA. His brother, Bert, served as a pilot with Bomber Command and had the distinction of taking delivery of RAF's first operational Lancaster. He was later taken prisoner after the famous daring low-level daylight raid on Augsburg, for which he was awarded a well-deserved DFM.

Follow this left fork now, and the road takes us past the Beacons to Cleddon Moor. When I was young this really was a moor and quite dangerous in the winter. Despite the wetness it was nevertheless set on fire several times by picnickers. The last occasion that I recall was when some builders set it on fire building an emergency water tank in case the moor caught fire.

The road forks again here and again we take the left one. The road narrows as it passes Cleddon Hall, where Bertrand Russell lived and I believe was born. When I was young, an elderly General Hobkirk and his wife occupied it. Further on, we come to a cluster of small cottages, and just below these are the beautiful Cleddon Falls, as they drop down to Llandogo.

Just here is Cleddon House, where the poet Keats lived at one time. When I knew it a Captain Tyler, a distant relative of Charles Rolls, owned it. He had been badly gassed during the war and lived on a small service pension and a bit of inherited money. My father rented twenty acres of land from him for many years. It was a condition of the tenancy that we supplied him with milk; so, every morning it was my job to deliver the milk, a mile round trip in all weathers, before school. He and his wife were a friendly couple, and within his means he tried to be a village squire. Every year at Christmas he donated a book to every child at Catbrook School who had not lost a day's schooling during the year. They had six sons – all much older than us – although I think the youngest was a contemporary of my brother, Sid.

Every one of them served in the armed forces during the war: one an RAF Squadron Leader, was killed over Germany. Captain Tyler's gardener was the bugler Wilson Morris whom I spoke of earlier.

Returning to the last fork, we take the main road to Llandogo and Tintern. There are a few cottages scattered alongside this road, and all formed a part in my life as I grew up. On the left was a cottage occupied by a rather grumpy widower called King and his son, Tom, who was a close friend of my brother Stan. By a strange coincidence, Mr King died the same night as Stan; consequently Tom lost his father and best friend on the same night.

Just below this on the right was another cottage, made mostly of corrugated iron. This was the home of Wilson Morris, his wife and daughter Betty – a girl of about the same age as my brother Bill. Wilson was born in 1900, and being a Territorial he was called up in 1939. Shortly after he was sent to the Western Desert where he served for about three years before being returned to the UK as unfit for desert service, but was still kept in the army. His wife got bored with life and 'took up' with another man. When Wilson was demobilised in 1946 he had no family (Betty had moved out in disgust), no home and no job. If he had been born a few months earlier he would have been too old to be called up. His elder brother, George, a Corporal in the South Wales Borderers, was killed in Flanders in 1917.

Wyeswood

It's a dark wet November afternoon. A woman, clutching a babe in arms, is running through the downpour with four small children towards a cabin-style house, set in a partly cleared wooded area. Back on the road, some hundred yards from the house, stand two furniture vans, while the drivers and their mates glumly survey the prospect of carrying the entire contents of the vans to the house. Unknown to them, however, a neighbouring farmer has seen their plight and hastens, with two farm carts and a labourer to help.

The woman with the children was my mother, the babe is myself, the children are my brothers. This was the first sight that any of us except my father had had of the place that was to be the family home for thirty years, and the place where my mother would end her days. When I asked her many years later about not seeing it before they moved her reply was, 'Do you think I couldn't trust your father?' Her one stipulation when my father was looking for a smallholding was that the house had to have a water tap in it.

The four small children were my brothers: Sid, eight, Ted, seven, Stan, five, and Bill, three. The neighbour was Danny Edwards of Ninewells Farm, and this was to be the beginning of a friendship between the families that would last for a quarter of a century, and almost to a marriage between them.

'Wyeswood' consisted of a timber cabin-style house built by a Mr Chandler, the previous owner, who had lived for some time in Canada. The house was surrounded by woods and some rough fields formerly known as 'The Bathwood'. I think that the old name and that of Ninewells referred to old Roman baths, as there certainly was a Roman-style bath in the orchard of Ninewells Farm; unfortunately, I know of no official history of the area or of the neighbouring village of Catbrook.

What then brought my father to Wyeswood? To answer that I have to go back a few years. Briefly, he had previously been employed as a herdsman, but all his life had been dogged by severe rheumatism as a result of rheumatic fever in his youth; indeed at one time it was so bad he was known as 'the man on two sticks'; it was so severe that the army wouldn't take him, even in 1916.

Although very happy in his previous employment, where he had a good job and a large house, his employer, a Cardiff shipowner with more foresight than most, decided to retrench his businesses and sell the farm. A part of the farm was later incorporated into RAF St Athan.

So at forty years of age, what does a redundant herdsman do? Bearing in mind that any business he went into had to be something my mother could keep going if he was incapacitated, he opted for poultry farming. Not only was this a lighter form of farming, it was also something that required less capital.

This then was the chain of events that brought us to Wyeswood on this wet November day some six months before the great financial crash of 1929. It wasn't the most auspicious time to start, but with the unfailing support of my mother, make a success of it he did. How? Obviously, hard work played a big part in his ultimate success, but also he was in the right thing at the right time. Poultry farming in the past had been a subsidiary part of a farm carried by the farmer's wife, but this was a time of great change in all facets of agriculture. Most counties had an Institute of Agriculture to train young farmers and to advise existing farmers on how to take advantage of the new practices.

Always forward-looking, my father took to this immediately and created a niche by breeding high-quality stock, and being able not just to sell eggs for the table but also for other farmers to hatch. He also sent chicks and hens all over the country and was proud of being only the fifth farm to be an officially recognised Poultry Breeding Station, all this being aided in no small measure by his regular successes at the Monmouthshire Egg Trials: in 1936 he 'swept the board', taking every prize there was.

This didn't of course happen overnight; fortunately he had been able to purchase Wyeswood outright, so every pound left over after keeping us all went into the business. Of course all I know of the very earliest days is what I have been told. I do however recall him felling trees and putting up fences. Another memory that lingers is him 'turning the eggs'. He started with three incubators. In these were placed 150 eggs which took three weeks to hatch. Every twelve hours these eggs had to be turned individually to ensure equal warmth to all parts of the egg. After some years he was able to buy a 900-egg incubator, in which turning the eggs was done by turning a handle. Although hatching was a regular event it was always exciting to see the beaks poking through the shells. All this meant that my father's working day lasted over twelve hours every day of the year. He deserved every shilling of his success.

The increasing number of poultry houses he made and built measured his progress. When my father found a design that suited him he would buy one and then get Mr Evans, a local carpenter, to make more to a similar design. Mr Evans told my father not to waste his money in letting him do all the work but to get a hammer and work with him. Like so many carpenters at that time, he was also the local undertaker; he told my father of how, during the great flu epidemic of 1919 he had difficulty in getting help for the funerals. On one occasion he had only four people, including the vicar, to bury the deceased.

In all this my mother was no idle onlooker. Almost everything we wore she made. Shirts and trousers were sewn on her trusty Singer sewing machine, while jerseys and socks were all knitted in the evenings. In addition to all this, the cooking had to be done on a small range. Gooseberries, raspberries, blackcurrants, plums, some home-grown, some bought at the Friday market – all went into the pot to make enough jam for the coming year. She also made all our butter. I can see her now, churning the cream and reading a book.

Until her last illness I cannot ever recall my mother ever sitting in the evenings without her knitting. Even when we had grown up and left home she turned to Fair Isle knitting for everyone, daughters-in-law and grandchildren included. She also managed to read a book, and later listen to the radio, all at the same time.

Most of what I have written of the early days is of course what I have been told. I have some hazy memories, mostly of trips to

Monmouth or with Dad about the farm, or going to Tintern Station and being frightened to death by the railway engines. One of the highlights of going to the station was when we called in on Fred Howells, the blacksmith. Fred was a farrier and until the war always shod father's horses. Seeing him standing in his forge, hand on hip, pipe in one corner of his mouth as he pumped air into the fire and as the coals started to glow, he presented to my child's mind an almost satanic appearance. Here he and father would discuss world and local events. It was here that I probably first heard the word 'Hitler'.

Apart from business, they were the greatest of friends. Father helped Fred to start poultry farming, and he, on the other hand was always available to help with advice and help on mechanical matters. When tragedy or trouble struck he was the first to help. He was one of the central characters in my early life. By the late thirties, mechanical progress particularly in the timber extraction business, saw a great reduction in the demand for Fred's services. Traditionally timber had been moved by special wagons similar to a gun carriage that required very large strong wheels. The wheelwrights made the wooden part of the wheels. The iron tyres, known as 'bands', were made and fitted by the blacksmiths, this was a very skilled job for which the blacksmith had to make a circular fire to expand the band so that they would fit the wheel; water was then poured on the iron so that the metal would shrink onto the wheel.

Hauling the timber by these methods was a hard job for both man and horse. It was quite a frightening sight to see these huge horses slipping and sliding, sparks flying from their shoes and the metal brake, when the laden wagon was going down a steep hill. By the late thirties work had fallen off so much that Fred went to work on the construction of a munitions factory at Dinham. Ironically, the factory was being built over land that included the farm where Joan was born.

Catbrook

Describing the village is difficult, indeed I don't even know if it could be classified as a village. Its origins are obscure, and its area almost impossible to delineate. It had only one main street, and that had only a few houses on each side. The school, which I attended for nine years, was built in 1876. It was known as an 'Elementary' school, and served the educational needs of the area for 113 years until its closure in 1989. Until 1944 children stayed at the school from ages five to fourteen, the exception being those who took the scholarship to either of the two Monmouth Grammar schools. I was due to sit this exam but my parents decided that owing to my health problems that it would be better if I didn't go. I have very few long lasting regrets in life, but not being able to go to Monmouth school is one of them.

The children are now bussed to a new school at Trelech.

The church was in the field opposite the school. It was built of corrugated iron and was known as The Mission Church of St John. There was a church hall in the same field as the church, also built of corrugated iron. The Rev. King tried to get a few events going there; it was also the headquarters of the Catbrook Brass Band. The conductor was the same Mr Roberts who kept the post office. Every Christmas morning they would tour the whole district playing carols. They would even make a special trip to include us; needless to say, they were well rewarded for their efforts. Sid got himself a cornet and joined them when he came home to farm Whitelye. When he wasn't about, I would get the cornet and try to play the thing. My efforts were rather spoilt by my dog, Joe, who would plant himself in front of me and howl throughout my performance. This is probably the reason why I never developed a musical career, although others may say it was due to a complete lack of any musical talent.

Prior to the church being built the spiritual needs of the area were provided by two Methodist chapels. These were not however in the village 'centre', one being in Whitelye, over a mile away. The other was in Parkhouse, again over a mile away from the village. Marriages and funerals took place in Trelech, over two miles away. There was one exception to this: Reggie Williams was the first person to be married in the church, which, I suppose, must have been in the thirties.

Even the origin of the name 'Catbrook' is shrouded in mystery, although there is a village of Catebrook near Bristol, I know of no connection between the two. Even the local dialect was different from the surrounding villages, being more akin to the dialect of the Forest of Dean – with whom there existed a great enmity.

There was no real industry in the village. With the exception of Ninewells Farm, the land was split into smallholdings, many of the owners having a full or part-time job. The 'main' street boasted a general store. Here we could buy groceries, sweets, cigarettes, boots and shoes, cattle and poultry feed, plus other items too numerous to mention. There was also a butcher's shop kept by a Mr and Mrs Howells. Their son John was amongst those Catbrook men who were killed during the war. Further up was the post office, also selling sweets and tobacco. This was kept by a Mr Roberts; he always suffered bad health and died during the terrible winter of 1947. It was two weeks before the coffin could be taken to the church, and only then with the assistance of the council snowplough.

The woods provided employment for quite a few men. Some were employed as timber fellers, others in timber extraction. One of these was a Mr Edwards who also lived in the main street; he was the last man to use a traction engine for extracting timber. Fed up with trying to get good coal during the war, he gave this up, and used a tractor thereafter. Another character involved in this trade was a Mr Kinsey. He drove the last chain-driven Scammell tractor ever. He went away on Mondays and lived all the week in a portable cabin. On his retirement the Scammell went into a museum.

Many lads went to work for the Forestry Commission on leaving school at fourteen. Their job title was 'beetle catcher', for which they received the princely sum of ten shillings (50p) for a 48-hour week. Most got the sack after two years when the wages went up; they were, however, able to claim unemployment benefit, as the two years' employment had given them the necessary 104 stamps on their card.

The rest of the men, if they had a job at all, worked in the quarries, in Chepstow shipyard, or for the County Council on the roads.

The other public building in the village was the Memorial Hall. Built of wood, possibly from old army huts, it was a practical memorial to the men who had served in the First World War. It was here that we had the Christmas and royal occasion parties. During the war, regular dances in aid of the Red Cross or the Welcome Home Fund were held here. It was still in existence in the 1980s but I believe that it has been replaced.

Parkhouse was a hamlet of its own, being on the back road from Trelech to Tintern. In my day there were only a few houses there, but it did have the only pub in the area, which meant a long walk for the thirsty folk of Catbrook. Particularly in wartime, it was the only social centre we had. The inn consisted of a small bar and a lounge for the ladies; in those days women did not go into the bar. That however all changed when the Americans came; after that the girls were allowed in the bar with us. It was to be many more years before women felt happy about going into a pub on their own.

Inside we played darts (we had a good darts team), cribbage and indulged in the old rural pastime of making ribald comments about neighbours' gardens or farm work. Woe betide the farm worker who failed to plough a straight furrow. Worse still was the fate of the man who got a bend in a line of corn when drilling. He had to live with that until the harvest – another example of one's peers being better than the boss for upholding standards.

After all this time it is difficult to remember all the characters that make up the warp and weft of a village like this. The major families were the Williams, Richards, Watkins, with a few Harrises and Phillips thrown in. One Williams family lived near the school. The eldest – Greta – became Greta Swain; Greta was one of those women who struggled to bring up her children on her own while her husband was away.

The eldest son was a bit of a lad when a youth. He was in court for some misdemeanour when he was offered the choice between going to 'borstal' or joining the Royal Navy. He chose the navy; he was away for many years, returning home only after his ship was torpedoed off Tobruk in 1941.

Another son was Elwyn. He was a great friend of Ivor Crocket, and both were keen Pentecostal members, both leaving when they decided to join up. Ivor was another of Catbrook's war causalities; Elwyn went on to survive the war and many bombing missions over Europe.

Of the many Watkins families I recall three in particular. First, there was Marcus Watkins and his family, who were mostly of the same age as us. Dave was our last war casualty. 'Bomber' (real name forgotten) was a great friend of Bill's. I remember having a crush on Grace; I was about eleven at the time.

Further up lived Mr and Mrs Horace Watkins. Their eldest son, Frank, was probably the best friend I had in my last years at school and mid-teens. The family were especially kind to me at the time of Stan's death. Frank and I left school at the same time. Horace was a bricklayer and on leaving school Frank was apprenticed to him. I remember going to see him on the Friday at the end of his first week, only to find his mother bandaging his fingers, which were raw from handling bricks, and the lime mortar, which was used a lot in those days.

Despite all that was happening around us we had a great time growing up. Together we cycled all over the area, from Monmouth to Chepstow and all the villages between. Frank's father being a strict Pentecostal, he was not allowed to go to dances or the cinema, which restricted us a bit. Not that these vetoes ever came between us, nor did we ever discuss them. Parents were parents and we just had to accept their whims.

As soon as we could we graduated to motorbikes, which not only extended our range and 'street cred', but also led us down some risky roads. One of our greatest problems was lighting. Fortunately, the bikes didn't need a battery to start, but one was needed at night, and here was our great problem, as batteries were virtually impossible to get just after the war. The law, however, was more lenient then, and required only that one should show a white light to the front. Many times have we travelled with one of us holding a bicycle lamp over the driver's shoulder. On a few occasions I managed to get home by following the sky between two rows of trees. Frank had a beast of a bike then, a 600cc 1928 long-stroke Norton; the bike was so long that four of us could – and did – ride on the thing at the same time.

The fourth member was Bert, three years younger than Frank. He too went in to the building business. When he was doing his National Service I was working in a shop in Monmouth, and his mother would bring a weekly parcel to me to wrap up for her. By coincidence Bert's daughter married the son of Joan's cousin.

Before I go too far up this road I must backtrack to the church and take the other road up the hill. Just up this road lived another Williams family, of which my schoolmate Ivor (Conk) was one. Mr Williams (Jacob) was a widower who lived there with his two other sons and his parents. I had an odd sort of relationship with 'Jake', as he was more generally known. Firstly, I was just a small boy who was also a friend of his son. It was in this house that I first saw a football coupon. Conk was amazed that I didn't know what the football pools were (they hadn't been going many years then). In those days they were the one hope of the unemployed to escape to something better. Sometime about 1942 he moved to a cottage further up the street. By this time the two elder sons were in the forces, the eldest served for four years in the Western Desert. This was when our relationship changed; from now on he treated me as an adult, and would give me his son's letters to read when I visited Conk on Sunday mornings.

Just opposite Jake's house lived a Mrs Lloyd. Her son, Ben, was at school with Sid, and when he left school he joined the Rhodesian Police Force. Because of the war he was unable to visit his mother until 1950. By this time she was very old, so she decided to sell up and move out with him; my Uncle Tom, who had just retired, bought the house from her. This had an echo over fifty years later, when the wife of a friend of ours visited us in Spain and recognised the Catbrook School plate on our wall. 'That's my grandfather's school!' she exclaimed – and indeed she was Ben Lloyd's granddaughter.

From here the road turns left at the top of the hill, continues past the Memorial Hall to Broadstone – otherwise known as Windy Corner. Here we turn right to the little hamlet of Cicelyford. At the outbreak of war the army stationed a searchlight unit here. They were withdrawn after a few weeks when they realised that the Germans would hardly regard this collection of six houses a threat to the Third Reich.

Schooldays

However all this changed for ever in September 1933 when I started school. Everyone remembers their first day at school, but I doubt if any of you can visualise what an event this was for me; to do so you have to realise what a sheltered and isolated life I'd had until then, with no near neighbours and no children nearby. Girls were a totally unknown species. However, off I had to go, half a mile to school – up the hillside, across the field, then across Danny's muddy orchard to the road, which at that time was still a sandy track, only being metallised some years later. It was a journey I was to make four times a day (Mum insisted that we had a cooked meal midday) for the next nine years.

The school consisted of three classrooms, infants (five-eight years), middle (eight-ten years) and top class (ten-fourteen years). In my time the infants' teacher was a Maudie Reynolds, who came to school on a motorbike. A kindly woman who was ideal for the job, it was she who taught us to read and write; not an easy task when many homes didn't possess a book.

In addition to teaching, the school also doubled up as a local library. Every two weeks a van from the council would deliver two crates of books to the school. These were not only for the pupils, but were available free to all adults in the village – a service much valued, especially by my Mum.

The teacher for the middle class was a Miss James. Sadly, it is only much later that I have realised how much I owe her. According to report she wasn't properly qualified, but nevertheless she was a very good teacher. In the two years I spent with her we learnt all the basic rules of grammar, and how plants grew, including trying to make a kidney bean plant grow the wrong way. Her great love was music, rather wasted on us (especially me!), but she did try. This was all done without any teaching aids except a blackboard. So, 'Jampot' – if you are watching in that celestial schoolroom, a sincere if much belated tribute.

The upper class room (Standards Four to Seven) was presided over by the headmaster. We had quite a few of these during my time. First came a Mr Jenkins, who ruled with a rod of iron or, more precisely, a hazel stick cut from the hedge. He was followed by a Mr Griffith, a man of small stature instantly dubbed 'Goliath', who battled for four years until going on to better things. I remember him most for his insistence in making us observe Armistice Day; he himself had served as an ambulance driver on the Western Front.

A forward-looking man followed, who rejoiced in the name of Makepeace. I enjoyed school under him. He was a most remarkable artist and lined the walls with drawings of the leaders of various countries; it was he who got us to dig the trenches in the playing field. During lessons he used to brew some horrible concoction over the stove to alleviate the stomach pains caused by being severely gassed during the war.

He was followed by a Mr Morris, the best headmaster we ever had. Later he became commander of the local Home Guard.

This was a time of great social changes, one of which was the introduction of the milk-in-schools scheme. Bill and I were involved in this from the beginning. The scheme started in a modest way with milk being provided for two children from TB-ridden families. It was our job to collect bottles of milk every day from Danny Edwards and carry them to school. No one was happier than us when the government brought in a proper scheme to provide milk for all, at one half-penny a bottle. TB families got it free.

It must be difficult for people to realise that before the last war certain families were blighted by TB; children would live to their late teens and then die.

One family like this was the Voyces, who were later rehoused to Llanishen. At this time the County Council gave a watch to every child who didn't miss a day's school for five years. One condition was that it had to be the same school, so Enid Voyce (a girl of about my age) walked to Catbrook for a week – a round trip of ten miles. Coming from such a background this was a most remarkable and courageous effort.

Walking to school was a must for everyone, many walking much further than we had to, and rain or shine we did it, such was the respect for the law and the benefits of education. Another occasion that I recall was a boy walking two miles in his football boots because his school shoes had collapsed and his parents had to wait until his father collected his dole money at the end of the week before buying a new pair.

In case anyone thinks that the village children had it easy, fate had a way of evening things up. Few if any of the village houses had a water supply (and didn't until the middle fifties!) so when the local children got home they had to pick up a bucket and carry the water home from the well at the bottom of the village green. Whatever else we lacked we sure got plenty of exercise!

This formed the background to my childhood. It was at school that I learned to make friends, and the first I remember was Ivor Williams, otherwise known as 'Conk' (don't ask). Left motherless as a baby, he lived with his father and grandparents. When young we were quite close, and I think it was Conk who got me to ride a cycle, play darts and later drink beer. Through him I got interested in football, especially our local team, who in the late thirties carried all before them; whether this was skill or their reputation for robust play I can't say. There was one occasion when a lady in the crowd told Reg Williams, who had just brought an opponent down, 'Kick him in the guts, Reggie!' I'm still not sure whether it was sportsmanship or the close proximity of the ref that stopped Reg from carrying out the advice.

Still on football, it was when we were returning from Chepstow after Catbrook had won the Hospital Cup that I first had a taste of beer, something that has stayed with me ever since. Little did we know that it would be six years at least before we saw those blue and white shirts in action again.

Life, however, was not all school. In 1934 my brother Sid left, as did Ted the following year; both worked at home for a while before leaving. Sid went to farm work until going to Usk Agricultural College and Ted went off to work with my uncle in London. At home, as general prosperity increased, in 1935 my father was able at last to extend the house; in the same year we celebrated King George's Jubilee with a carnival and high tea in the Memorial Hall, and watched the oldest inhabitant plant a copper beech tree on the village green.

The year of 1936 was to see more momentous events with the king's death, and then, at the end of the year, the abdication. For the latter event we went to Ninewells Farm to hear the king read his abdication message. This was the first time I had ever listened to a radio broadcast. It was almost one of the wettest summers on record. The farmers were in desperation trying to get the hay harvest in.

Although I didn't perhaps realise it, these events heralded the beginning of eventful and tumultuous times. Next year we were to see the coronation with yet another carnival, followed by another tea and the planting of yet another tree. At home my excitement knew no bounds when I found that we were to have a radio to hear the events in London. Having a radio in those days was a little more complicated than now, although aerial poles were no longer needed. Being in the country the radio needed two rechargeable batteries (accumulators) and a high tension battery, bringing the total cost to about twelve pounds, equal to three or four weeks' wages.

In addition, the accumulators needed charging every two weeks. The shop that supplied the radio sent a van to collect these as required for sixpence a time. The young man that used to do this was later to give his life serving as a Wireless Operator/Air Gunner with the RAF.

Apart from school, what was I doing? Like all those on a farm we had our jobs to do before and after school, and like all youngsters on Saturday mornings I had to get enough kindling wood for the following week. One of father's friends was a Jewish butcher, a Mr Krototsky from Cardiff. My father did business with him for many years; his worst habit was to visit on a Sunday afternoon when, one of us – mostly me (being the smallest) – had to crawl around the dusty poultry house to catch whichever hens he wanted. This, combined with Sunday school, was not conducive to a pleasant Sunday afternoon.

In the holidays we had of course to help with things like the hay and corn harvest. Although Bill and I played together when younger, later on we drifted apart as Bill, being all of three years older, found friends of his own age. I tended to be on my own, not that that worried me; together with my faithful fox terrier,

Joe, I wandered all over the woods and fields that surrounded us. On one Good Friday when I was ten I even walked to Llandogo, along the Wye Valley road as far as the abbey, before returning home. I must have walked at least seven miles with Joe following me all the way. The surprising thing was that it was only when I was late for dinner (dinner was the midday meal) before my parents started to wonder where I might be. This was not an uncaring attitude; apart from road traffic there was nothing to worry about, and even that was very light.

After I learnt to ride my cycle I started to cover greater distances. One of my friends was Bill Charles of Cicelyford, whose father owned two steam traction engines. In the winter he would take the threshing machines to various farms. In the summer he was employed hauling timber from the woods. Bill had a good talent for drawing, although entirely self-taught, he even won a few newspaper competitions. What he might have achieved we will never know, as there were few opportunities for lads like him. Sadly, his father died when he was thirteen, so there was no money left to help him anyway.

This then was the pattern of life at this time. Generally things were improving for everybody; there was more work for all and more money to spend. This was not to last. Already the clouds of war were building up; my parents grew more worried as they discussed the situation. All of us, even the children, were affected by the Munich crisis. When Chamberlain promised 'peace in our time', my mother was so relieved she wrote him a letter of thanks. Although deep down they doubted if the peace would last, the horrors of the Great War were still a vivid memory. My early memories of Chepstow were not of the castle or the river but of the men in 'hospital blue' walking the streets, often talking or crying to themselves. At this time Chepstow had a large military hospital used solely to look after the shell-shocked remnants of the war. No one wanted any more of that.

Reality broke through six months later when the government introduced compulsory military service for all twenty-year-old men. It was supposed to be for six months' training only; in the event it was to be for six years or more. Sid was one of those affected; hoping to avoid this, he joined the Territorial Army. All to no avail, but the army did agree to postpone his training for a time so that he could help to get the harvest in.

As children we didn't think of horrors, we only saw the excitement. In June we all got our identity cards. There were no computers, no charge, just a simple code of four letters and three numbers, or four if there were more than nine children. Later we were issued with gas masks. Thankfully these were never needed, but again, memories of the last war were fresh and, quite rightly, no chances were taken.

Preparations were also being made for the reception of evacuees; all householders were told how many children to expect. Although there were hitches when the time came it worked smoothly. One of the hitches occurred in our village. Generally most folk were 'church' (C of E) or 'chapel', even if they didn't worship much. The trouble came when the first lot of children billeted locally were Roman Catholics. The nearest RC church being eight miles away, they were unable to attend mass. Exchanging them with an equal number of other children solved the problem. This caused some upset, but things soon settled down again.

Despite what has been said since, those who had evacuees billeted upon them accepted the new arrivals with kindness. Obviously there were exceptions and difficulties. The children had to get used to bucket toilets, and the older ones to helping to carry the household water from the well and living without electricity. The foster-parents had to get used to these strangers from what was at that time almost another world, and for those who had never had children of their own it must have been quite traumatic.

The foster-parents were paid a meagre allowance for keeping them; some parents made sure that their children were provided for, others sadly paid nothing and left it to the foster-parents to clothe the children and some totally forgot them and just enjoyed themselves.

And so the hot summer wore on, while rumours of war filled the air. In July Bill left school and in August I had the only holiday away from home that I ever had as a child.

War

It is a hot day late in August. Two people are sitting in the bus waiting for it to leave Ross. One is an eleven-year-old boy full of excitement at returning home after a holiday; the other is a middle-aged woman looking with sadness at the newspaper hoardings warning of the imminence of war.

The woman is once again my mother. I had just had two weeks' holiday on my Uncle Bennet's farm at Weston-under-Penyard. It was an odd sort of household. My Aunt Julie had died some twenty years earlier, together with two of her daughters, in rather strange circumstances – what, I have never really known. The housekeeper was my cousin, Violet, living there with her two young daughters. She had been tragically widowed two years previously when her husband died as a result of a bee-sting.

Also living there was my cousin Charlie, who at that time was recovering from having one leg amputated as a result of an accident some years previously. The final member of the household was Charlie's son, Francis. I was not aware of this relationship because Charlie had had a divorce, something almost unthinkable in those days. Both Charlie and Francis were very good to me. Charlie used to take me for walks to his favourite spot in Penyard woods, from where we could see over large tracts of Herefordshire. In a way he and I had an affinity, as he also suffered from a stammer. During the war he worked in Birmingham where he met a blind lady who later became his second wife.

Violet was having a hard time. My uncle was a tight-fisted man and, knowing that my cousin had nowhere else to go, he made sure he got his pound of flesh. Among other things, Violet had to bake their bread; I can still taste that oven fresh bread spread with her own butter and fresh raspberry jam. Uncle was not very approachable. I remember him most for being the first person I ever saw using a cut-throat razor. I watched him a few times, waiting for him to make a slip.

49

All this was very quickly to fade into the background as the world events unfolded and our lives suffered a cataclysmic change. The first day of September started the same as usual, but by nightfall our lives had changed for ever.

As I walked past Captain Tyler's study on my way to deliver the morning milk to the kitchen, I saw him on the telephone. As I walked past he stopped me to give me a message to tell Sid, Don Howells and Brian Richards (two men from the village) that they were to report to their units immediately. Full of importance, I rushed home to pass on the message, and that is how the first men left our village for the 'duration' (Duration of Present Emergency, the government catch-all for any regulation).

It is interesting to compare these men's fortunes. Sid was the only one of the three to serve overseas. Brian managed to transfer to various home regiments. Don fell down a dock in Cardiff he was guarding, thereby sustaining a minor injury to his foot. This meant he missed the draft that sent Sid to India; he spent the rest of the war either going AWOL or doing punishment for it.

By evening my parents knew that war was inevitable. They went to bed knowing that all they had worked for, and the future they had hoped to give their family was about to disappear. In its place was a period whose length was unknown, a period of fear and worry for the future. All this was against a background of memories of the First World War, during which my mother lost her brother, Will, in the Battle of the Somme. My father's brother, Jim, was killed in the carnage of the Battle of Loos. In addition my Uncle Stewart lost an arm and uncle Bill a leg. Now they faced the prospect of yet another major war. This was supposed to be the century of the Common Man; but by mid-century the common man had been killed and mutilated on a scale unknown since the dawn of history.

Whitelye

In 1938 my father took the boldest step since buying Wyeswood when he bought Whitelye Farm. This was a forty-acre mixed farm about a mile by road from Wyeswood. The farm was mostly grassland, with some arable, but all in very poor condition due to many years of neglect. Although the storm clouds were gathering I don't think Dad realised that the bad financial times would soon end and he was, in fact, in the right place at the right time.

Although it boasted a Methodist chapel, Whitelye itself was neither village nor hamlet, more a straggling settlement. It is situated about 1½ miles north-west of Catbrook; the top of the farm bordered the road between the two. At the opposite side lived a redoubtable lady by the name of Miss Harris, a well-known figure in the area, as she walked everywhere with her two Scottie dogs, one white, one black. A fearless defender of 'rights of way', she was a thorn in the side of anyone who barred her path. During the war, when Ernie Williams legally diverted a footpath because he was compelled to plough up a field, she nonetheless continued to march through a field of much needed wheat.

Apart from the chapel there was also a shop kept by another Miss or possibly Mrs Harris, who until the war drove a donkey and trap around the villages.

Although the farm was ostensibly for Sid, because of the demands of the Territorials he spent less and less time there. When Sid was called up, Father was left with the job of running the three farms without him; Ted, not being required in London for a few months, helped out, as did Bill, who had just left school.

The War Years

The outbreak of war changed life for everyone. Some got through it without a tragedy close to them. For some, it was an opportunity to make a lot of money, but for us it was traumatic from the beginning: six long weary years, years of hope, despair, sadness and sometimes joy, but nothing was ever the same again. For me the six years was a period when I moved from childhood to manhood. Age made little difference; we had to grow up quickly in those days!

Sid served for six weeks in the UK before being sent to join his regiment (1st Battn South Wales Borderers, then stationed in Cawnpore). One week's leave was all he had, and it was April 1945 before he would return. All these years later I can still see that dull October morning as we lined up to say goodbye before he got into Danny Edwards' car to catch his train in Monmouth. Only much later did I realise what was going through my parents' minds with the memories of World War I still fresh. This was the last time we were ever together as a family.

The war to us as children was, certainly at first, a time of change and excitement. For my parents, mindful of the carnage of the previous war and their own personal loss, a time of hope for better things was replaced by a time of concern and worry.

At first it was all excitement, a glorious autumn with an extra two weeks' holiday to settle the evacuees into their new homes. When we returned, our headmaster – a WWI veteran – set us older boys to digging trenches in the playing field in case we got bombed; quite why the Germans should decide to bomb our little country school was never quite explained, but it did provide a novel playground until the authorities decided that we were more likely to be injured by ourselves than the enemy, so we had to fill it in again.

The forties started with the coldest winter for many years. All day we could hear the eerie sound of crashing trees, as the branches were unable to bear the weight of ice upon them. The 'Phoney War' ground on, and Ted returned to London. Sid seemed to have settled in India, and my parents battled with the blackout and adjusted themselves to having to run the three farms.

Then came June and the threat of invasion: more excitement for us, more worry for the adults. Father took to keeping a loaded shotgun by the bed and when the call came joined the Local Defence Volunteers (LDV, sometimes known as 'Look, Duck and Vanish'), later named the Home Guard). In recent years the Home Guard has become something of an object of ridicule, due mainly to programmes like *Dad's Army*. The reality was very different. Although at first they were armed with ordinary shotguns, by August rifles were issued. My father had an ancient Canadian 'Ross' rifle which he kept well locked away. What he didn't know was that I knew where the key was kept, so one day when he and Mum were out I got the key and played soldiers, including fixing the bayonet. That part was easy; getting the bayonet off was not so easy. For half an hour I struggled to get the thing off, all the time in a cold sweat in case my parents came back before I found out how to remove it.

Wyeswood was the lowest edge of the of the Catbrook Home Guard area. This part of the Wye Valley was classed as a coastal area, so our farm was used as an arsenal. Amongst other things were boxes of hand grenades; I used to pick them up, wondering what it would be like to actually use them, fearful all the time that the pin might fall out. Somewhere by Ninewells Pitch they also buried Molotov cocktails, and as far as I know they are still there. When Bill joined, he had to meet the coach at the bottom of the hill. However, the hill was too steep for the coach, so the troops had to get out and push. After this happened a couple of times Bill thought it a better idea to wait at the top of the hill and watch his comrades do the pushing.

Few people today realise what being in the Home Guard meant. Drill meant turning out two nights a week plus Sundays, this coming after working at least nine hours a day for 5½ days, plus often an hour's travelling each way. Would they have been effective? It is said that the quality of an army depends on the quality of its sergeants. The sergeants in the Home Guard were some of the most battle-hardened men in the world. They were the veterans of the Somme, Loos, and the entire list of WWI war battles. Could any army ask for better? Some people think it was a waste of time and effort. I can only say, what would have happened if Hitler had developed the V-1 and V-2 rockets twelve months earlier? D-Day might never have been possible. The colours of the 10th Battalion were laid up in Trelech Church.

As the beautiful summer went on people adjusted to more severe wartime conditions and shortages. 8 August was notable for three things: the Battle of Britain started, it was my eleventh birthday, and the day my life changed for ever when I went down with rheumatic fever. However, I duly recovered, went back to school and life went slowly on. Before the war about twenty or thirty young folk with nothing better to do, and no money to do it with anyway, would congregate at the bottom of the village. By the end of the year only a few remained. Within this time all were either working or had been called up. By the end of the war over sixty men from Catbrook served in the armed forces, and not a few paid the supreme sacrifice; the last being David Watkins, who sadly died of wounds just after VE day. They gave all for a country that couldn't even give them a water tap in their houses. By 1945 I was, at seventeen, probably the oldest 'young man' in the village.

After the Battle of Britain, the needs of total war gripped the nation. The London Blitz started giving Mum more worries about her London relatives. By night we could often hear the German bomber planes as they followed the River Severn to Birmingham and the Midlands, or sometimes nearer as they bombed Bristol. It was this that caused us a lot of problems, as the poultry food came from Avonmouth, and the suppliers had to send us the raw materials with instructions on how to make it ourselves.

So one year merged into the next. Christmas was very low-key, few presents and no goodies in the shops, the blackout making life even gloomier. At Christmas Ted gave up working in London and came home to work in Monmouth until his call up to the RAF in May of 1941.

It was later in the year that the shortages really started to bite, especially for those on low incomes who could not afford the off-ration extras. Sadly, most of these were the wives of servicemen with children, who could not work or shop for extras as they lived in the country.

It was then that Mum came into her own as a 'black marketeer'. On Fridays she would use eggs or butter as bartering items to obtain extra food. The government also allowed extra rations for harvesting or other seasonal farming activities. Mum scoured the adverts to make sure she got all she could, and then gave it all away to those families who would have gone short.

This had an echo many years later at Mum's funeral, when I thanked Greta Swain for her help; her reply was, 'If it hadn't been for your mother we would have starved during the war.' Could anyone have a better epitaph?

During the year, because of animal food shortages and the demands of Whitelye, Dad had to give up poultry farming and concentrate on other crops for the war effort, often at short notice. In farming, production is planned at least on a yearly basis, but not in wartime! I remember in the spring of that year Dad was suddenly ordered to plough and plant potatoes on a field that was only rough pasture. Despite my father's protests that the field was useless for such a crop, if the War Ag said 'plant', plant you did. In the event I think we got fewer potatoes out than we put in.

As the autumn leaves started to fall, so more family changes took place. Stan had left to work for the War Ag as a tractor driver, which often meant that he was away for usually fourteen hours a day, leaving Bill as Dad's only help on the farm. Ted was in Warrington training as a metalworker.

Christmas that year meant no presents, as toys and games were in very short supply. Clothes and sweets were strictly rationed (Joan recalls feeling at the foot of the bed and finding nothing there). It was also my last Christmas at school. There was no food for parties, and the only presents were for the evacuees, which obviously caused much envy amongst the rest of us.

This, although sad, was a small matter, as the war took a turn for the worse with the Japanese attacking Pearl Harbor, Malaya and Hong Kong. Whatever else happened the war certainly improved our knowledge of geography. Early on, Father bought a large-scale world map; by this time there was something happening almost everywhere.

This then was our life as the new year, 1942, dawned. Although we lived in times of great changes, no one could ever have envisaged what the year would bring to us as a family. For me it was the year that I would leave school and start work, a year in which I would have to grow up very quickly. At that time most boys wore short trousers until they left school at fourteen. For me and quite a few of my friends this sign of adulthood was limited to a pair of bib and brace overalls. I think it was for my birthday that I got my first pair of grey flannel trousers – ten clothing coupons if I remember correctly.

May was the month that the family fortunes went downhill. Early in the month Ted was sent overseas. It was to be six long months before we knew where he was and that he was relatively safe and well.

It was at this time that Sid's battalion was rushed from Iraq to the Western Desert to join the Eighth Army and the battle for Tobruk, where after four weeks of continuous fighting almost the whole battalion was killed or captured.

It was a bright and sunny July morning at Wyeswood. I was home with my mother when Tom Evans, the postman, brought the letter from the War Office. As soon as Mum saw the buff envelope she knew it could only be bad news. I can still hear her crying, 'Oh dear, oh dear!' as, with shaking hands, she struggled to open the letter to find that her eldest son was posted as 'missing'. There is a widespread belief that relatives of war casualties were always notified by telegram; this was not so. Relatives of officers were notified in this way, but relatives of 'ORs' (other ranks) were notified by letter. A leaflet of advice accompanied this letter. There was a case at Llanishen when the first thing the wife of a sailor saw when she opened the envelope was a leaflet headed 'advice to widows'. Whilst the discrimination was totally indefensible, notifying all relatives by telegram after a major disaster like Tobruk, where UK casualties totalled 30,000 men, would have been virtually impossible for an already overloaded telephone system.

Mum's first reaction was to rush over to Whitelye to tell Dad what had happened. So began many anxious months of waiting for official news of Sid's and Ted's survival.

The first news we had of Sid was when his name was included in a broadcast by 'Lord Haw-Haw' (the British traitor who was broadcasting for the Germans). Joy however soon turned to worry when the War Office told us that the German information was not always true. It was Betty Edwards (Danny Edwards' daughter) who had listened to the broadcast who told us the news. This was the first time we knew that there was a romance between them. The next news came from a Vatican representative who had visited the prison camp and passed the message that Sid was safe. Not long after this we had a postcard from him.

It was in early November that we had the first letter from Ted to tell us he had arrived in India en route for Burma, where he was to spend the rest of the war. Almost all of his time was spent on a forward airstrip, where all supplies had to be airlifted in, as they were surrounded Japanese occupied territory. It was from this airfield that the famous 'Chindits' took off for their second strike into enemy country. Before moving to the airstrip he fought at the famous Battle of Kohima. Being out of ammunition, his unit was airlifted out twenty-four hours before the final victory; the first land defeat the Japanese had ever suffered.

On this memorial is inscribed those famous words:

When you go home, tell them of us and say,
    For your tomorrow, we gave our today.

Ours was not the only family to suffer in the Catbrook area at this time. Ivor Crockett, one of a well-known Whitelye family, was killed fighting in Burma. Sadly, he was not the last of the young men of the village to make the great sacrifice before the war finished.

By August I had left school and started full-time work on the farm. What a time this was! No school, long trousers, wages (five shillings a week), and on the way to being a man. All this was overshadowed by greater events culminating in Stan's death in the November.

Looking back over the years it is surprising how little I remember of Stan as a child. I think he was a bit of a tough at school, but that was part of survival in those days. Like all of us he had to work on the farm before and after school, and I can recollect nothing but kindness from him. He was a rather self-conscious person, but he had an open cheerful nature, from which came his nickname – 'Smiler'. This was everyone's name for him, and how he was remembered. Even after forty years I met an old schoolmate who still called him that. Because of the age difference, sadly it was only in the last few years that we became close.

When the war broke out he went to Usk on a tractor-driving course and afterwards worked for the War Ag until his death. The work pattern after 1940 was almost always dawn-to-dusk; certainly during the winter months, he never saw his home in daylight. Often his work took him thirty miles from home, which he travelled by pushbike until he bought a Coventry Eagle 250cc motorbike. He was only able to use this for a year until the private petrol ration was abolished in 1942. When he applied for an essential worker's ration, some callous official scrawled 'pushbike' over his application! To add insult to injury, he was called on to explain why he wasn't turning up for Home Guard duty.

Despite the long hours he did manage to find a girlfriend. She remained faithful to his memory for many years, and it was a rather poignant occasion when, many years later, I went to her twenty-fifth wedding anniversary party.

It was about this time that Stan and I got to know each other better. Almost every night we played draughts together as we listened to the radio – that is, if he came home. Very often, especially if the weather was bad, he would stay overnight with a friend who had more compassion than the officials. So long were his working hours that after his death my father found several unopened pay packets in his pockets.

This then was a person whose life was to be so tragically and needlessly cut short. It all happened because some 'mechanic' had bodged a repair on the transmission to a combine harvester, and then bodged up the safety cover. Stan thought the cover might fly off and injure someone, so he took it off. On the last afternoon that he would have been working on it he caught his trouser legs in the transmission, which shattered both legs. As a result he died at three the next morning; his last words were my name.

Stan's death was the most terrible thing that ever happened in my family especially as it happened when it looked as if things were getting a little better. Mum's birthday on 25 November was a happy time; Sid was officially 'safe' as a POW and after five long months we had had a letter from Ted in India. Then, after the Battle of El Alamein even the war was going our way.

Even now as I write this, sixty-two years later, I can relive almost every detail of that awful week. The evening of the 26th, when we first learnt of Stan's accident, my parents were fetched by the police to go to the Monmouth Hospital. Frank Tansell came to spend the night with us and tried to soothe our fears (it was many years later that he told me that he knew how serious it was). I can see now Father stooping by the bed to tell me that Stan had 'gone', but it was only when I got up and saw Mum huddled by the fire, racked with grief, that the awful truth hit me.

How we got through that day I do not know. Dad had to write to friends to let them know what had happened, and as always it was Fred Howells and his wife who were first to help and comfort. I think I spent most of the morning stroking Joe (my dog).

In the afternoon Dad sent us over to Whitelye to feed the cattle (animals have to be fed, whatever the heartbreak), and what an awful foggy November day it was.

The next few days we struggled on. Being on a farm meant there was always something to do, until on 1 December Stan was laid to rest in Trelech churchyard. As was normal in those days, it was a 'walking' funeral, with the mourners walking behind a hand-drawn hearse. I travelled with Danny Edwards in his car for the two miles to the church, where the local Home Guard provided a guard of honour. Stan's friends carried him into the church where, in happier times, he had been a choirboy. As the coffin was lowered into the grave, Bill and I broke down as we realised the awful finality of it.

I cannot end this without paying tribute to my father who was such a rock for all of us at this time and in the long months that followed. Without him I do not think Mum would have survived; despite his own grief, it was his strength of character that got us all through.

If this year was the depths, the next year wasn't much better for my parents. Bravely, they struggled to come to terms with their loss and to cope with running the farms under wartime conditions, and the demands of the War Ag. Its word was law, dictating what crops were grown to replace food supplies that were lost by the U-boat campaign.

The Red Cross was doing a terrific job at this time in providing support for the families of POWs. In addition to the regular food parcels sent by the central organisation, families were permitted to send one personal parcel every three months. In Monmouth this service was run by a Mrs Richardson, who was a tower of strength to relatives, especially as letters were few and far between or, in the case of Far Eastern POWs, virtually non-existent. Life must have been little short of hell for these people. Whereas we could expect about a letter a month from Sid, these relatives were 'lucky' to get a letter a year. How these people kept their sanity I do not know. Later, as the news of the Japanese ill-treatment of their prisoners seeped out, the relatives' despair and fear must have been terrible. The waiting was especially hard for the wives of these men, particularly those with children. In addition to trying to live on the niggardly allowance paid by the government, they had to cope with the loneliness of solitary living. Once the children were in bed, and the blackout curtains drawn, every hour must have seemed like a week. Many of these women suffered all this only to find, late in 1945, that their husbands, for whom they had waited so patiently, had died some years before.

In June, Bill joined the Home Guard – the last of the family to wear uniform. Later he went to work on a farm in Mitchel Troy. Apparently the authorities regarded one man and a boy sufficient for 100 acres, so Bill left home sometime during the summer. I believe that Bill was never conscripted because it was thought our family had had enough.

August was 'all change' for us. Mum and Dad thought that Mum would be better if we moved to Whitelye. Unfortunately, Dad had let the farmhouse, so it was necessary to swap houses with the tenants. However, the tenants didn't want to change, so Dad had to take them to court to get them to agree. So on about my fifteenth birthday, we moved house. This was great for me as we were less isolated. I was nearer to my friends and we didn't have to walk over to Whitelye twice a day. Sadly though, we had not been there long before Mum realised she had made a mistake; but of course there was no going back until after the war. I remember my father telling me, in despair, of his difficulties at this time, and of how my mother would often lie awake in the night, sobbing. Always in the morning she would put on a brave face, and I would never have guessed the state she was in if my father hadn't told me. He himself must have been desperate to have to confide in me.

Also in this month the Italians surrendered. We had high hopes of Sid coming home, but the Germans had other ideas and quickly moved the prisoners to Sagan, Eastern Germany (now Zagan in Poland), where he was to remain until 1945.

Communications with Ted were now much better. Although he was stationed in the Burmese jungle the use of microfilmed letters improved, and in one case we had a letter only five days after it was posted.

After the move life settled into a pattern that would last until the end of the war. Every day we waited for the postman. The work on the farm went on. War, though often exciting and dramatic, also brought a lot of sheer boredom. Mum gave up letter writing after Stan died, so it was left to Dad and me to write the weekly letters to Sid and Ted; no one today can realise what a job that was. First of all we had to use standard letter forms, which we felt duty bound to fill up somehow. Imagine writing a letter to someone who rarely replies! The subject matter was limited. For instance, one could not write about the weather (might help the enemy), friends who were killed (alarm and despondency), food or other shortages (U-boat campaign); if you did, the censor would chop it out. I resorted to very long spaces between words to fill the form up. As an example of the censor's stupidity, once, when Sid was in Iraq he wrote in a letter, 'Terrible place, this, not worth being here if it wasn't for the oil.' The censor duly blacked out the word 'oil' – after all, the Germans may not have known that there was oil in Iraq...

For me, in my early teens there was little amusement to be

had. Winter evenings could be especially dull. The newspapers consisted of only one sheet, so they didn't take long to read. Mum used to bring books from Howe's lending library on Fridays. I thought at that time that farming would be my career, so to this end I would have books sent from the National Library of Wales. As I grew older I started going to dances and, although I was underage, pubs. Occasionally I would go to the cinema, but cycling eight miles to the cinema and eight miles back in the blackout rather took the shine off the enjoyment.

Another aspect of life for young people was the severe clothes rationing, which must have been particularly galling for the girls. The only new suit I had during the war cost twenty-six coupons, which made a sizeable hole in my yearly ration of fifty-two.

Townspeople mistakenly thought that country folk didn't go short of food. This however, was not the case. Although most had gardens, food doesn't grow by itself, and cultivating the garden was something that had to be fitted in between long working hours and the demands of the Home Guard. Additionally, the unrationed extras such as fish never seemed to be in the shops on market days. Some of the villagers supplemented the rations by planting a row of potatoes in a farmer's field. This was not only a wartime event; it was a practice going back many, many years. Traditionally the potatoes were planted on Good Friday. My father never charged for this; the unwritten rule was that the villager would turn out to help with the haymaking.

All farmers and some cottagers kept a pig or pigs (two was the maximum allowed by the government). Pig-killing day was always a major day in the rural calendar, and although not the great fiesta that we now see in Spain, it was nevertheless quite an event. Firstly the pig was hauled, squealing and pulling, from the sty to the bench. There two men and the pig-killer would lift the pig onto the bench, where the slaughter man would cut the pig's throat. As soon as the pig was dead it would be rolled off the bench and a straw fire lit around it to burn off the hair. The carcass was then hauled to a shed, where it was strung up on a beam for disembowelling. Next day was the ceremony of cutting up the pig. It was an old country saying that everything of a pig could be eaten except the squeal. This was certainly true: the sides were cut up for Mum to cure by salting down for a month; and the liver was made into those wonderful faggots. The rest of the meat was shared between us and our neighbours; they in turn would repay the compliment when they killed their pig.

Fred Howells always killed our pigs until the war, when Father had to find someone else. The only person he could find was a man of about seventy (incredibly old to me). One year when I was thirteen I arrived home from school to find Dad ill with the flu. When I told the man this, all he said was, 'Don't bother, we can do it ourselves.' We were able to do this because he used a humane killer – a pistol! When we got the pig to the killing spot he told me to hold the pig's tail, while he at the other end wrapped a cord around the pig's snout, which he held with one hand. The pistol he held in the other hand, and at the right time fired it to kill the animal. Imagine my feelings while I'm holding the tail... There is this old codger, holding a reluctant pig weighing around twelve score (a score is twenty pounds) with one hand, while holding a pistol aimed at my potential manhood with the other! Next year, I had a little more confidence, although I think Dad held the tail that time. After all, I had more to lose.

The Dawn of Hope

Slowly, hope was returning. Everyone knew the Second Front was coming, indeed had to come, as people were getting so very war-weary. Everywhere there were dumps of vehicles and stores, and convoys filled the roads. One very new experience for us was the sight of coloured American troops in the streets, who were as warmly welcomed as any other soldiers. The only racial troubles were caused by white Americans, who were amazed to see British girls chatting to blacks. For the rest of us, anybody who would help to get rid of Hitler was welcome.

So at last the great day came – a day of hope and sadness too, as we all knew that the final victory would only come at the cost of much loss of life. One month later the V-1s started to hit the South of England causing Mum to worry again about her family in London.

For myself I was growing up rapidly. On my sixteenth birthday I had to cycle to Monmouth (eight miles) to register for essential work, then back to spend the afternoon and evening working on the corn harvest. So with rising hope we carried on through the rest of the year, culminating with my going down with rheumatic fever again over the Christmas period. This was to be the beginning of a traumatic and difficult time for me; it was an event that would make me reshape my whole life. As I slowly recovered I had to come to terms with the fact that I would have to abandon all thoughts of pursuing an agricultural career and look for something away from the land. It was to be some years before I would get into a settled into a regular career again.

With Christmas over, we knew we were on the last lap, at least as far as the war in Europe was concerned. In January 1945 we were told to stop writing to Sid, as the postal service in Germany had broken down. The worry now was, what would Hitler do with the POWs? Would he massacre them or let them return safely? This was answered for us when, in early April, we received the telegram from Sid to say he was safe and well in Allied hands.

It was a gaunt, rather haggard figure that alighted from the train that bright sunny morning, almost staggering under the weight of his kitbag as he stepped into the glory of a Wye Valley springtime. Once again the line had brought a warrior home. The journey that had started that October morning, 5½ years before, was nearly over. It had taken Sid to a dozen different countries, from a dull English autumn, through France, by troopship to India and finally to Cawnpore in the United Provinces, which would be his 'home' for the next year and a half.

Army life, at first, was very much as it had been before the war. First the new intake had to be integrated into the regular unit. Fortunately they had just returned from the North-West Frontier, so Sid and his mates were spared having to fight the Pathans and the Afghans.

After initial training, Sid was sent on a course to become the unit vehicle mechanic. The reward was to be promoted to the dizzy heights of Lance Corporal. This distinction was removed when he had a furious row with an officer, who reminded Sid that he was in the army now. Sid's reply, that he was a civilian in fancy dress, didn't endear him to the regular officers in command.

The Tenth Indian Division, of which the SWB were a part, were moved to Iraq to become Tenth Army, based in Basra. They were originally destined for Singapore but the Japanese found out. In a cunning ploy to outwit the future enemy, the War Office sent the 11th Division instead. It seems as if Sid was destined to be a POW, as that would have been his fate if the original plans had been carried out.

Their stay in Iraq was to be a brief one, after six months they were rushed to the Western Desert. Here they were thrown into the desperate battle to save Tobruk – and desperate it was! Under strength, 550 men instead of 1,000, which was the normal complement for a battalion, they were thrown into the fight. He spoke of the frustration of seeing their shells just bouncing of the German tanks, and the time they were sent 4,000 yards over flat sands to attack a German airfield… with bayonets. Fortunately, the Germans had withdrawn, so they were spared for another day. On a lighter note he also spoke of a neighbouring unit that captured a mobile Italian brothel, complete with staff. Whether they were able to avail themselves of the ladies' services he never said.

After a few weeks they were ordered to withdraw. The CO decided to split the battalion; half were to go deeper into the desert, the others towards the sea. Most of those sent into the desert survived. The rest got bogged down in the sand and were captured.

After three days in their trucks, with only the food and water they had with them when captured, they were shipped to Italy. For the next fourteen months they were to 'enjoy' the delights of the Italian Riviera at Campo 52. Although Sid never spoke of having to work when in Italy, conditions were not good. It was five months before he was issued with a pair of boots. The guards would also steal from the prisoners' parcels anything they fancied. By contrast, this never happened when they were in German hands.

When the Italians surrendered in July 1943, everyone hoped that the prisoners would be returning home. Hitler had other ideas. By September, after a three-day journey by cattle truck, they were in Stalag VIIIC in Silesia. Like most servicemen who had suffered badly, it was to be many years before Sid told me much of his experiences. Most of what he told me was the last time I saw him, six months before his death in 1995.

Life in the Stalag was no picnic. Under the Geneva Convention, prisoners must receive the same rations as base troops. So low were the rations that they would not have survived without the Red Cross food parcels. The German guards had to resort to buying or cadging extra food. For the Russians, who shared the camp with them, neither option was available. Every day the Russians would bury twenty or thirty of their men who had died of starvation.

Whilst the Germans carried out their responsibilities under the Convention, they also exercised their rights: namely, that other ranks could be put to work. Sid's work was working in a cement factory; he avoided farm work by calling himself a mechanic. He said after that the idea of working outside in a Silesean winter was not overly attractive.

He was charged once with committing sabotage (he had). If it had been proved he would have been sent to Auschwitz for sentencing. It is not generally known that some British prisoners were sent to work in that place. I visited the camp in 1994 and actually saw the place where he would have been executed.

He made two escape attempts while he was in Silesia. On one occasion he and two mates were out for ten days. Someone overheard them talking and called the police. Despite several days of interrogation, during which he gave only his name, rank and number, he was returned to camp.

All this time the Russian armies were getting nearer. In mid-January 1945, the Germans decided to move them to the west but not by train. This time they would have to walk. They had three days to get themselves together. Sid and two mates decided to make a sledge rather than carry their few belongings. I was rather touched to find, on the last occasion we met, that amongst those belongings were the letters I had written.

So began a long and painful journey, a journey that would last forty-four days through the bitter hell of an Eastern European winter. Forty-four days without having a decent meal; once they even went nine days without any food at all. One man was nearly shot for running into a field to get a raw swede. Sometimes, he told me, they were able to break out at night and get food from a farmhouse. He always said that the German women were good to them. When they opened the door and saw who was there, they would pull them in, give them a bowl of soup and bread, and then send them out. All this without a word being said on either side. 'Where were the men?' I asked him. His answer, 'All in the army.'

As they neared western Germany, Allied planes were seen in the sky. This led to the worst day of the journey, and for Sid probably the worst day of his army service. By this time he explained that they were now wearing German uniforms, as were millions of troops and forced workers throughout Germany. Seeing a line of men on the march, one the pilots decided to shoot them up. That day they lost fifteen men; one of them was a Corporal Richards from Newport. They had served together for 5½ years; he was killed as they lay together in a ditch. What must have been his thoughts as he lifted himself out of that ditch to realise that his comrade was dead! A man who, for all that time, had shared the hardships, danger, and near starvation that had been their way of life for so long. It was one of the terrible ironies of war that Richards should lose his life in such a way, only two months from victory and so near home.

Finally the survivors reached their last Stalag. This was not be a rest camp. After six days in camp, which Sid remembered most for collecting a clout from a rifle butt for attempting to steal bread, they were ordered to move again. Sid didn't fancy this much; indeed, he doubted whether he could survive any more marching.

After three days' marching back into Germany, he managed to escape. Together with two others he got out of the barn in which they were sleeping and reached the sanctuary of a wood. For ten days they hid there, sustained only by a bucket of potatoes and, I suppose, some water. Here they lay, too weak to move, just listening for the sounds of the advancing guns. One day, as some German soldiers came near, one of their group became so hysterical that Sid and the other man had to hold his face in the mud to avoid detection. On the tenth day they could hear sounds of the advancing American troops. In desperation they decided to make a break for freedom, and after nearly getting shot by their allies (remember they were in enemy uniform), at last they were free.

It took another week before they returned to Britain, a week of American hospitality during which they made themselves ill coping with the food that the Americans lavished upon them. This then was the experience of the warrior who stumbled out of the railway carriage at Tintern, three weeks before the final surrender of the German armies. I was working in the fields when the taxi brought him home, so I can only imagine my mother's welcome for him. There was one final sting, however; while Mum went out to tell me he was back, Dad had to tell him that the girl he thought was waiting for him had married someone else.

For Sid and me, the six weeks' leave he had was a strange time. Apart from the excitement of the moment, and Sid's recovery, we had to get to know each other for the first time ever. As time went on he had become rather a shadowy figure to me. Sid, on the other hand, had left a child, only to be met a by person taller than he was. While the people of Catbrook were celebrating the end of the war, there was sadness too, when the news came that David Watkins had died of wounds during the final push.

For us and for all those with relatives in South East Asia Command (SEAC) and Japanese POW camps, the war was very far from over. It must have been hell for these people to see all the celebrating while they didn't know if their men were alive or dead.

We had one lucky break here. In April the government announced that all units in SEAC would be allowed to send one man on leave to the UK for one month.

Mum and Dad's joy can only be imagined when we were told that Ted's name had come out of the hat. At last we were together again. Sadly, however, their joy was tempered by his ghastly appearance. Three years of living in the Burmese jungle had taken their toll. Thin and haggard, Ted's skin was a horrible yellow colour due to the anti-malarial tablets they had to take. For the first time he told us of when he nearly died from the disease when he had to spend three weeks in a 'base' hospital. The hospital had three wards, the intake ward, the serious ward and the 'coffin' ward where the fatal cases were taken for their last days.

For Mum it was as good as it would ever be, but with only six now around the table.

In June Ted flew back to India to rejoin his unit, ready for the push to Singapore. Soon the worrying started again, as they prepared for the attack on Singapore. However, the worry was to be short-lived, as the Japs caved in after the atomic bombs were dropped. This time we could all celebrate. Everyone's thoughts now turned to the return of the Far East POWs, and their families who had suffered so much.

It is sad now that so few people know anything of the war in Burma. Tens of thousands of our men died there: some in battle, some of disease. All of them, of all services, lived and worked in appalling conditions of heat and humidity, for years on end. Leave, if they got any, had to be spent in rest camps or Calcutta. Ted's unit was for a long time totally surrounded by enemy-held territory; on one occasion, four men who went to sleep on guard duty were found, in the morning, with their throats cut. All supplies had to be airlifted in; the beer ration was one bottle per man, per week. Mail was erratic, if there was any, though the introduction of microfilmed letters helped considerably.

This was the 'Forgotten Army'. Forgotten then, forgotten now. It is particularly poignant now, as the sixtieth anniversary of D-Day is being celebrated. Without detracting one bit from the great sacrifices of the men who served on that day, surely time could be found to honour the men who served and died in other campaigns.

15 August 1945 was the greatest day ever. After almost exactly six long, bitter, weary years, we were able relax and try to put our lives back together again.

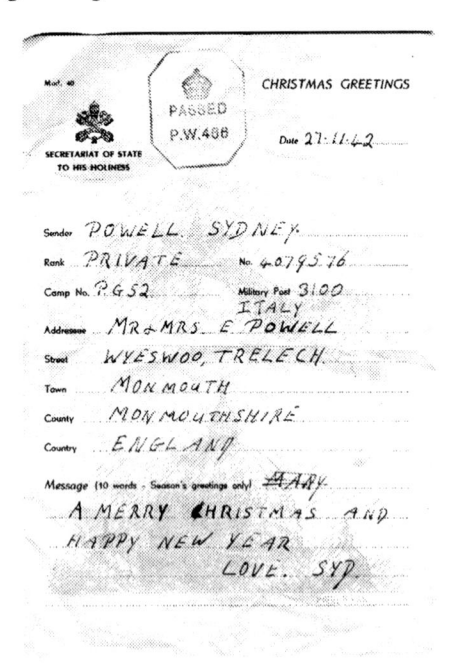

Only the second message in six months. Little did he know that his brother died of injuries that day.

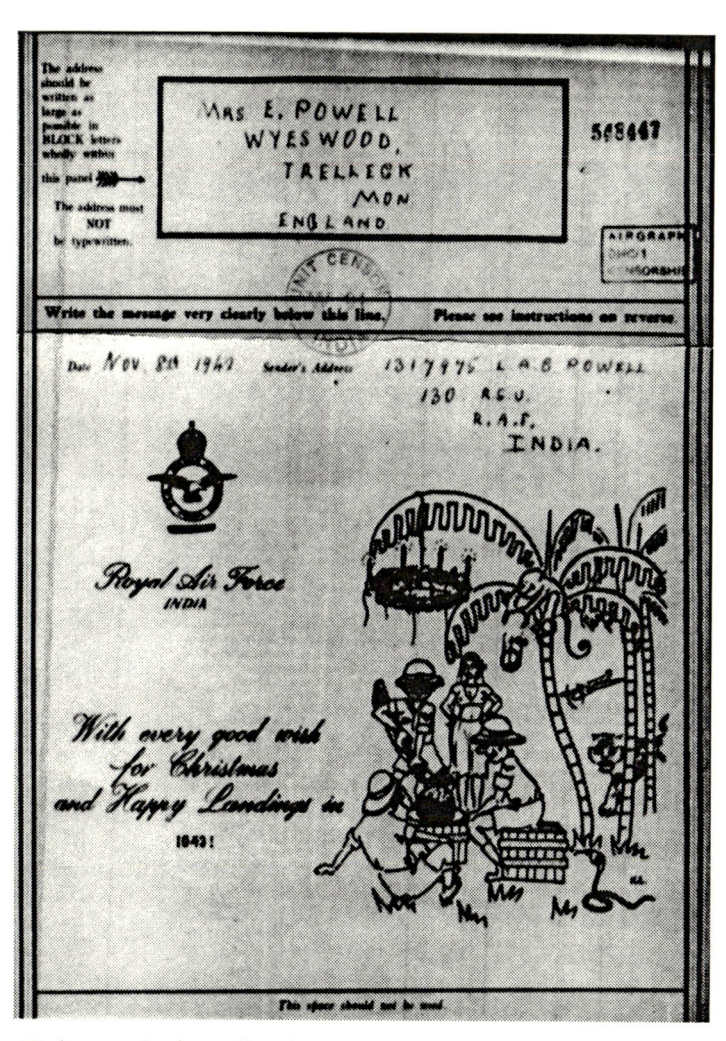

Early example of microfilmed message from far east servicemen, introduced in 1942 to improve morale.

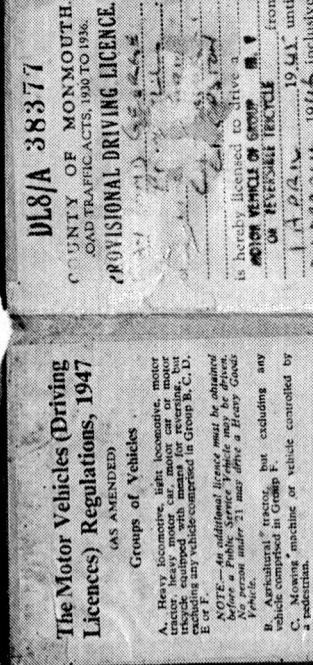

The Motor Vehicles (Driving Licences) Regulations, 1947
(AS AMENDED)

Groups of Vehicles

A. Heavy locomotive, light locomotive, motor tractor, heavy motor car, motor car or motor tricycle equipped with means for reversing, but excluding any vehicle comprised in Group B, C, D, E or F.

NOTE.— An additional licence must be obtained before a Public Service Vehicle may be driven. No person under 21 may drive a Heavy Goods Vehicle.

B. Agricultural tractor, but excluding any vehicle comprised in Group F.

C. Mowing machine or vehicle controlled by a pedestrian.

D. Road roller.

E. Track-laying vehicle steered by its tracks, but excluding any vehicle comprised in Group F.

F. Agricultural tractor which is a track-laying vehicle steered by its tracks.

G. Motor-bicycle (with or without side-car) or tricycle not equipped with means for reversing, but excluding any vehicle comprised in Group C.

H. Trolley vehicle.

K. Vehicle exempted from duty under section 12 of the Finance Act, 1936.

L. Invalid carriage.

D.L. 2B

DL8/A 38377
COUNTY OF MONMOUTH.
ROAD TRAFFIC ACTS, 1930 TO 1936.
PROVISIONAL DRIVING LICENCE.

is hereby licensed to drive a

MOTOR VEHICLE OR GROUP
OR REVERSIBLE TRICYCLE from

1.4.41 19 41 until
31 Mar 41 19 42 inclusive,
subject to the conditions prescribed in regulation 3 of the Motor Vehicles (Driving Licences) Regulations, 1937.
(See p. in book.)

Fee of
5/-
received.

THE TAXATION OFFICER,
"STELVIO,"
BASSALEG ROAD,
NEWPORT, MON.

Usual Signature of Licensee:

R. Y. Powell

Passport to freedom. One of the most cherished documents of my life.

Last Days at Whitelye

Despite all the excitement of the homecomings, the land is always there. My brothers returned to the services and we turned to the haymaking and the rest of the farming. Father didn't say much to me, but I know that he was very uncertain about what to do next. Sid had dropped a bombshell by saying he didn't intend to return to farming. Mum had no other thoughts than returning to Wyeswood as soon as possible and I, perforce, had to decide on healthier alternatives.

As soon as I was sixteen the previous year I had started to think of motorbikes. I started first by looking at the adverts in the *Farmers' Weekly* for Norman autocycles. These were advertised at £49, but only had a 50cc engine. Apart from any other drawbacks there wasn't much of what today would be called 'street cred' in one of those. Frank was one jump in front of me there. His father possessed a 500cc Norton, which he was sometimes allowed to ride.

I had to settle for something less exotic. In April I bought, for £22, a 1937 Excelsior 125cc motorcycle, and in the woods around Whitelye I learned to ride. Whatever we do in life 'the first' is the one we remember. How I remember that bike – reg no. CVB 506! This was to be my passport to the wide world out there that I had so long wanted to explore. Whenever I could I would polish and care for it. I have had many bikes and cars in the years since, but nothing as ever equalled the pride I had in the possession of that simple bike.

Learning to drive in those days was simplicity itself. Owing to the war there were no driving tests. Getting a driving licence was simply a matter of filling in a form and sending it, with a five-shilling postal order, to the council. What a magnificent licence that was! After seventeen one could drive anything – and I mean *anything*. Heavy locomotives, roadrollers, tractors, lorries, cars… and of course motorcycles. The only exception was track-laying vehicles. When I got my first licence I couldn't stop taking it out and looking at it every opportunity. Shortly after, the government decided that anyone who had held a wartime licence would not have to take a test, so, here I am, sixty years later, having driven all over Europe – and I still haven't taken a test.

Exploring very far was not really an option. Although the petrol ration had been restored, it amounted to only two gallons a month; small wonder that the likes of Len Hunt prospered.

Despite the smallness of the ration it was a wonderful experience to get out so easily and so quickly. I think Mum was a bit apprehensive at first but she got used to it. My longest trip on it was when I went to visit Uncle Sid some thirty miles away. My joy was to be short-lived, however, as after three months of proud ownership the gearbox cover broke. It was to be a whole year before I got a replacement.

Sometime during the summer Sid told Father that he would not be going back to farming when he was demobbed. Faced with this and having to operate from Wyeswood, Father had little option but to sell Whitelye and revert to poultry farming at Wyeswood. Before this the farm had to be sold, which was done in October, followed by the sale of all the equipment and most of the livestock. The sale took place on another of those dull, foggy November days. Farm sales are always sad affairs. All the implements that had been slowly acquired over the years lined up, the results all in the balance. Perhaps the saddest was trotting the horses up for prospective buyers. These were the animals on which our success had been built. One I had trained myself; both I had followed behind for many a mile as together we ploughed and cultivated the land. Now they would finish that day in the hands of strangers.

That, however, was not the end of things. When a farm changes hands, whether by sale or letting, there is, or was, a certain protocol to be followed. In the days of horses, tenancies changed on Lady Day, 25 March; but so as to allow the land to be ploughed, the incoming tenant was allowed to move the horses on Candlemas Day, 2 February. When a farm was sold the changeover was by mutual consent. Before the new owner could move in, the seller and buyer had to agree a price for the hay, straw, 'roots' (mangolds, swedes, turnips etc) and anything not sold at the sale. In addition time had to be allowed for the corn to be threshed and the grain removed or sold. It must have been well into the New Year before the last strand was broken.

The Aftermath

Just before VJ day, the tenants who had been at Wyeswood moved out, so once more we were back where it all started. Nothing, however, stays still. Ninewells now had a new farmer, so the old relationship was gone for good. Captain Tyler found the post-war cost of living too much, so he sold Cleddon House and moved into a small cottage near Trelech.

For me the move was not one that I welcomed. Life at Wyeswood there was lonelier than ever. Where only a few short years before there had been over a dozen young people around Cleddon, now there were none except myself. Once again I had the problem of getting out to see my friends or going to the cinema or dances.

I solved the problem by using Stan's old motorbike. This didn't prove too reliable, so I managed to acquire another identical model and cannibalised the two to make one rideable bike. It must be remembered that the maker's factory had been bombed flat during the war, so no spares were available. Getting enough petrol was always a problem, but I solved it to some extent by having two bikes. One of these I rode regularly, the other I insured but only licensed for one month every six months. I was then able to get another ration book (legally) for the princely sum of one shilling and sixpence (7½ pence).

Although Father had sold Whitelye, he still had some sixty acres to farm. During 1946 I still worked for him while studying at night to become a radio mechanic. Meanwhile being now a Registered Disabled Person, I was eligible for the government training scheme. This proved a long wait, as ex-servicemen had priority, but I was sent on a six-week rehabilitation course in Surrey, which took place over the Christmas/New Year period.

That year [1946] was a strange one. After all the years of tension, strain, and excitement, everyone tried to resume their old life. For those of my generation, we had no previous life to resume; we were children when the war started and young adults when it finished.

All young men that were fit had, of course, to do their National Service (eighteen months, later extended to two years) in one of the armed forces. Unfortunately, I was not one of them, but of course I had to register and have a medical.

For our family it was all change: in March, Sid was finally demobbed, some seven years since he had first put on uniform when he joined the Territorials. After a few days he travelled to London to take up a government training course and begin a new life in the building trade.

I think that it was in 1944 that Ted decided to make the RAF his career. After the Japs surrendered his unit moved through Burma to Singapore, where he spent Christmas. In the New Year he went to Japan as part of the British Commonwealth Occupation Force. After eight months he was repatriated to the UK and a home posting at RAF St Athan; only a few miles from where he was born and went to school.

The day I went to Surrey marked a turning point in my life. For eighteen years Trelech, Catbrook and the neighbouring villages had been my world. On that day I not only left my home and family behind me but also the friends that had played such a part in my growing up. Many of these I have never seen since, for even though I was to return home later, my path always led elsewhere.

Leaving home for the first time is a traumatic experience. It must have been especially so for my parents seeing the last of the family go; it was a bad day for my father, as coming home from market his horse dropped dead a mile from home. It was a day of excitement and trepidation as I went once more to Tintern Station.

The rehabilitation centre was designed to assess the physical and other abilities of persons recovering from injury or illness before recommending them for further training. The six weeks I spent there has affected me all my life. It being so soon after the war, most of the people there were ex-servicemen. Their disabilities came as quite a shock to me at first but I soon got used to men clumping around on a tin leg or men with no legs staggering about. Now at eighteen months after the war, some had spent a long time in hospital, and gruesome indeed were some of the stories that they swapped.

The one patient who affected me the most was a man who had lost three fingers off one hand and most off the other hand from suffering frostbite, after spending seventeen days in an open boat in the Atlantic. He told me that it had taken him twelve months to learn to tie his shoelaces, but he was still unable to tie his tie. The barmaids in the local pubs were used to helping these men, but one of them had a shock when this man had to ask her to take the money out of his pocket.

It was amazing to live among these men who had suffered so much, and would suffer for the rest of their lives, and not hear a word of complaint. Not one was bitter, not one said, 'Why me?' – and all thought that it was a worthwhile thing that they had done. This has had a profound effect on me all my life, for how can you feel sorry for yourself when there are people around like those men? That time also taught me how to live with and work with disabled people, and to realise that they are still ordinary people with a problem. When I was in the Young Conservatives one of our members was blind. Taking him home involved virtually walking arm-in-arm with him down the street. Many didn't like doing this as they stupidly thought it made them look 'queer'. My stay in Surrey knocked any such nonsense out of my head for good.

The winter of 1947 will be locked for ever in the memories of those who lived through it; not even 1963 matched it for the effect it had on everyone. The first snow started to fall on the 27 January and lasted for at least two days, with further falls during the ensuing weeks. In those days the country depended on coal for fuel and energy, and of course that had to be moved by steam trains. Within three weeks the whole country ground to a halt. Townsfolk did had least have electricity, but that was limited and whole areas would be cut off due to 'load shedding'.

To say that life in the countryside was grim would be understating the suffering that people had to endure. Owing to the state of the roads we had to walk six miles to get the family bread;

getting paraffin was a mere three miles to Llandogo, and carrying a four-gallon jerrycan over ice-bound roads is not funny. We were due to get a load of coal just before the snow fell, but as the snow had blocked the roads we had to manage with wood, of which we did have a good supply. When the thaw did come, Ted and I managed to drive into Monmouth, only to be told that all the coal had been commandeered for the flood victims.

Our worst experience was towards the end when a terrific blizzard blew up one evening. About nine o'clock, Father got worried about his in-lamb ewes, so there was nothing for it but to rescue them. It took us an hour struggling through snow three feet deep, in the face of a howling blizzard, to reach them. The object was to get them into a shed, but as the sheep had some shelter under the hay racks they didn't want to move far. For anyone who has never had the experience of moving a large reluctant woolly animal, through three feet of snow, in the dark, I can assure them it's not that easy. The labours of Hercules would be simple compared to our struggles that night.

Although life was far from easy we did manage to get out though and enjoy ourselves. In a perverse sort of way we enjoyed beating the elements; cycling over ice is not something to recommend. The struggles that others had made ours look easy. As an example, Joan tells of being snowed in for weeks and reaching the point when practically the only food left was porridge. Her father had a dairy farm and because the milk lorry could not reach them they had to pour the milk down the drain.

In some places the ground was so hard that graves could not be dug, and coffins were left in churches to await the thaw. For other farms, especially the hill farms of Wales and Scotland, the RAF was called in to drop hay to starving animals (no helicopters then). Life was hell for those folk in the remoter areas, but even they would agree that what came with the thaw was worse, as huge tracts of low-lying towns, villages and farms were swamped by tremendous flooding. Monmouth, Ross and Hereford were very badly hit as the Wye and Monnow Rivers burst their banks, the situation being made much worse when the water authorities had to open the dams in the Elan Valley. Years later householders could still show the waterline on the walls of their houses.

Much work has been done since then to alleviate the risk, but even so, Monmouth was flooded again in 2002.

After the floods came the sunshine. For months and months the sun poured down to make it one of the best summers of the century. The spring was most frustrating for me as I waited for my course to come through. Fed up with waiting and the lack of opportunities around Monmouth, I packed my bags again, went to London and got a job in a factory and moved into lodgings.

Once I had settled down I enjoyed my time in London. Fortunately, Sid was still in London as was my Uncle Bert, so I did have a fallback. I soon learned to stand on my own feet. My first digs in Perivale were horrible, but I found fresh ones in Ealing, coincidentally not half a mile from where our daughter Joanne is living today.

There was a great shortage of living accommodation in London at that time; however, my landlady did her best to help by cramming as many lodgers into her house as possible. We were a motley crew; looking back now I can only remember a few. There was George, from Swansea, a little older than myself, a few itinerants and Bill. Bill was definitely a 'one-off'. He was over twenty years older than me, and we struck up a rather unusual friendship. He never told me anything about his early life but he had obviously received a good education and thereafter blundered through life from one crisis to another. In 1937, during a 'down' period, he joined the RAF. Apparently all went well for a time. He even received a modest promotion until some misdemeanour brought him before the CO. Asked why he had joined the air force, Bill replied with his customary tact, 'I was out of work and the air force seemed a good job.' Years later he found that the officer had put a block on any further promotion. His language if anything went wrong was terrible – not loud, but a constant low muttering. The Landlady never liked him and after a bout of horseplay one night she chucked him out.

With George it was totally different; we went to pubs, to dances and anywhere he fancied I should go. It was then that I learned the difference in city ways. To anyone leaving a pub in the country everyone said goodnight. Here in the city one just walked out; and you didn't pass the time of day with everyone you met.

Almost every Saturday we went to an Irish club where they had terrific dances. I was completely naïve about North/South divide or the Catholic/Protestant enmity, which, I suppose, helped me to enjoy it more.

However, all this was soon to end; my training course came through, so in early December I left London for six happy months in Swansea; but that is another story.

Swansea and After

On a cold December morning, I waited once again at Tintern Station to begin another chapter in my life. I must admit that it was with some trepidation that I travelled that morning. Would I succeed? Would I get a decent job afterwards? Could I look forward to a steady life after all these years of waiting? All these thoughts were racing through my mind as I travelled. My mood lightened a little after Cardiff, when I met some of my fellow trainees; here I gained an undeserved reputation for generosity by handing my cigarettes around; the smiles soon changed when they realised that the fags were Turkish (all I could get the night before). We finished the journey in an evil-smelling cloud that seemed to permeate everywhere.

Swansea at the end of 1947 presented a drab and battered look. Everywhere there was bomb damage. What had been Oxford Street was now an empty space, used solely for the Saturday market. Just by the cinema was another empty space. Here a bomb had landed, and after the site was cleared, working on the principle that lightning never strikes twice in the same spot, an air raid shelter was built. Sadly this didn't work; another bomb did land there, killing over a hundred.

It was certainly an odd mixture that assembled there that day. Surprisingly, there was only one ex-serviceman – and he had the same disability as me. I and a red-haired fellow from Ebbw Vale were the youngest of the group. The oldest was a 45-year-old from Bridgend who I believe had worked in the coal mines. The day the course ended he took me into his house, ostensibly to meet his family; the real reason I think was to show me a photo of the Welsh 1905 rugby team (which included his uncle) which had played that famous (and still disputed) match against the All Blacks.

Of the twelve only about two or three of us genuinely wanted to be radio mechanics. Most were there not because they were really disabled, but had been unemployed so long that the local managers had to do something with them. Twelve months later only two of us were working in the trade.

In contrast to the previous year, the winter of 1948 was very mild. Early morning or after work I would often walk along the beach on Swansea Bay. If we were going to a dance we would often take a ride on the famous Swansea to Mumbles railway. Reputed to be the world's first public train service, it was, at that time, using curious double-decker coaches, affording wonderful views over the bay and towards the Gower Peninsula.

In early June we took our final exams. I think that all of us who were left passed; some had just dropped out, and one had had to leave for health reasons. I believe that he died before we finished the course. At last I thought I could get settled, and within a week had got a job with Len Hunt. What we didn't know was that in the Bell Laboratories in America three scientists had created the transistor, which made 50 per cent of what we had learnt obsolete.

In the meantime, what was the rest of the family doing? Mum and Dad had settled back in Wyeswood, carrying on with the poultry and sheep. At last they were able to enjoy a few years of peace and quiet. Sid was still working in London but had met a girl from Leominster, so in August came the first family wedding. Like everything else then it was overshadowed by shortages. I think Vera had a special allowance of clothing coupons to get her wedding dress. The reception was held in Vera's home, Mum contributing a lot of the food.

Ted had been posted to Blackpool as an instructor, where he met his future wife, Ina. They were married near Blackpool, but for some reason they had to pick the weekend when Blackpool turned on the Illuminations for the first time since before the war. Except for Bill, we all travelled up in one of Len Hunt's taxis. I had become friendly with the driver, Bryn. A real professional, he was always there when needed and absent when he thought he should be; in fact I had to almost drag him into the reception. He later set up his own coach service and developed a very good business.

Being the weekend it was, there was absolutely no accommodation to be had in the town. Mum and Vera had a bed, but the rest of had to sleep on the floor; the look on Dad's face had to be seen to be believed. Bill and I stayed on for the weekend; Blackpool was 'high, wide and handsome'. We went to the Tower Ballroom, drank quite a bit, enjoyed the fair, and were playing darts on the beach until the early hours.

This then was how the forties ended for us. Things were as they should be: all of us working, and our parents enjoying their later years. Although there were still shortages, rationing and controls, there was hope of better things on the horizon as we approached the latter half of the century in a blaze of sunshine. The decade ended as it had started, with one of the best summers of the century.

The Fifties

Towards the end of 1949 I realised that I was going nowhere with my present job. Despite the looming advent of television, the wage rates in the industry were pretty low so I decided to make a career change. The first day of the fifties saw me start work for the newly formed South Wales Electricity Board.

In April my new prosperity enabled me to buy my first really good motorbike – a two-year-old BSA. This reopened the world for me; no longer did I have to rely on buses or friends for work and pleasure, and I was able to take a more active part in the motorcycle club. The last event I took part in was a Festival of Britain rally; this involved driving over 200 miles of mid and west Wales – starting at ten o'clock at night!

We entered a team of three, one solo (me), one pair (Den and Alma) and one sidecar outfit (Jeep and Jeff Davies). Den and myself managed to get around without much problem; the highlight being having an early breakfast just as the sun was rising over the sea at Aberaeron. Jeep and Jeff had rather different fortunes. Having some problem with the sidecar outfit, Jeff stopped at a wayside garage for help. Jeep, feeling the effects of the previous night's beer, got out for a stretch. Jeff, having sorted the problem, jumped on the bike and drove off, leaving Jeep stranded. They both did manage to get to the finish, where we all met up again.

First question after signing in was to find somewhere for a drink; remember, this was Wales in the days of no Sunday drinking. We solved that problem by driving to Newport and brazening our way into the RAFA Club. There we were allowed to drink until 2 p.m. after which we were invited to join the members upstairs for the afternoon. Driving back home is the one and only time that I have nearly gone to sleep riding a motorbike.

I was driving home from Monmouth one Saturday night in early June 1951 when I decided to stop off at a dance being held in the Church Hall. Seeing a friend across the room, I went over to have a chat, only to find he had a girl with him who he introduced as his cousin. As soon as the music started I asked her for a dance… and that is how I met Joan, my future wife, mother of my children and life partner for over fifty-four years.

Joan

Born in 1931, Joan is three years younger than me. Although she was only nineteen when we met she had managed to have quite an eventful life. Born on a dairy farm in Caerwent, by 1937 her parents must have been looking forward to a pleasant if hard-working lifestyle. By now the Milk Marketing Board had been established, providing a guaranteed market and a monthly cheque for all dairy farmers.

This sadly was not to last. The clouds of war were then gathering there as elsewhere, and somewhere in Whitehall some deskbound official decided that this fertile happy spot was the ideal place for a cordite factory for the Royal Navy. Dozens of farms and houses were razed to the ground. Smallholdings that were created for the veterans of the First World War were destroyed for the Second. The disgraceful thing was that, despite millions of pounds and years of effort, the factory was so late that it contributed nothing to the war effort.

Obviously, all this caused terrific upheaval and distress. Not only did Joan's parents have to find a new home but a new farm as well. Joan's father managed to find a farm of about a hundred acres lying under the Graig Hill, situated roughly midway between Monmouth and Abergavenny, and about three miles from the family home in Skenfrith.

The change must have been a terrible time for Joan's mother. In Caerwent she had a modern home with hot and cold water and within easy reach of Newport. At Nant-yr-Ych she had a rambling fifteenth century house that had at some time been a mill. They did have a cold water tap in the house, but there was no hot water system. The house was damp, the floors were stone flags, and for cooking there was just one open fire with an oven attached, which like all of its kind, was liable to smoke or send showers of soot into the frying pan.

As well as having the house to deal with, she also had to arrange a new school for Joan and contend with all the problems of living on a remote farm in wartime, which involved two evacuees as well. Tragically, all this was too much for her constitution and she contracted tuberculosis; unfortunately she found herself pregnant at the same time. With all these problems the doctors advised a termination – a rare thing at that time. She must have been a very desperate woman to agree. As a lifelong Roman Catholic, this went against all her beliefs.

This, then, was the scene when she underwent the operation in Hereford that November day; sadly, it was not a success. After some days she suffered a pulmonary embolism and died in November 1945 at the far too early age of thirty-nine. She was buried in Skenfrith churchyard, the graveside service being conducted by the same priest whom had both christened and married her such a short while before.

Obviously this had a traumatic effect on Joan and her father. For a girl to lose her mother at such an age is always difficult, and having no siblings, Joan must have felt a responsibility to her father. When she was ten Joan passed the 'scholarship' exam for Monmouth School, quite a distinction in those days; but the war intervened once again, so instead she went to Abergavenny High School. Her mother's death unsettled her, however, so she left school to work at home. I don't think leaving school worried her too much, though. She always preferred the outdoor life to the academic, even if it did involve cooking dinner for a full-size threshing gang of some fourteen men!

Apart from a spell of about eighteen months working as a telephonist in Lyndhurst, this was Joan's life until that wonderful day in October 1952 when we were married in St Mary's Church in Monmouth. I related earlier how we travelled to Tintern Station that day to catch the train for our honeymoon; a week later we returned on that same line. Perhaps it was fitting that this occasion was the last time that I would travel on the line that had been such an integral part of my life for so long.

Shortly after we got engaged, I realised that the unions had too tight a grip on things at the Electricity Board for to me make progress, as I had not had a full apprenticeship, despite being as good as many of my workmates. Perhaps I should have realised this earlier, but having no experience of a unionised industry I thought that I could get on.

With this in mind I left the Board and got a job managing a radio and cycle shop in Monmouth. This went pretty well until a few weeks after our honeymoon I twisted my back whilst putting up a TV aerial and pulled a ligament. Unfortunately the specialist who treated me just followed the fashion and declared that I had a slipped disc. It was only after twenty-five years of quite regular pain that I got a proper diagnosis and cure.

So, what was the treatment? First he laid me face down on the bed, then took a running jump and punched me in the back where he imagined the problem might be. The pain was terrific. After the treatment (he called it manipulation) he tried to make me walk. This wasn't exactly my best thing at that moment. Next was Plan B: encase my whole body from hips to armpits in plaster for three months. What a way to start a married life… and in reply to the obvious question, I'm not telling!

Christmas, though perforce quiet, was not an unhappy time, despite Joan finding herself pregnant a few weeks before. Joan was working at home; I did what I could and in addition I had my sickness pay. By the end of April I was out of plaster and recovering from the 'treatment'. My employers had already told me that they had been unable to keep my job open for me, so, as spring arrived, I had no job and a pregnant wife. Casting about for something to do, I thought I would try the dairy business, something I followed for the next year and a half.

Wendy

It was two days after my twenty-fifth birthday, on 10 August 1953, that Joan gave me a late birthday present – our first child, Wendy. She came into the world at six on a bright and sunny morning, and that has been her nature ever since. She was born in the Victoria Cottage Hospital in Abergavenny, which like all hospitals then, was ruled with a rod of iron by the matron. This lady regarded all patients as backward nuisances whose sole aim in life was to disrupt the smooth running of her hospital; relatives were even further down the social scale, beings to be treated with scorn and contempt.

The birth went without complications. I was at work at the time, but I was able to phone the hospital to get the great news at seven. It was to be evening before I was able to visit and see our firstborn for the first time. There wasn't an awful lot to see as she weighed in at less than seven pounds. There is, without doubt, no experience more awesome than seeing for the first time this person that you have produced together, and the nervousness at the realisation of the responsibility you now have. Joan was in hospital for ten days rather than the two weeks that was normal for a first child then. It was the doctor that overruled the matron to allow her to go home; apart from going home early, the matron didn't like patients going home on Fridays because she considered it unlucky!

I got Alban Martin, our local taxi driver, to bring Joan and Wendy home. During the trip – like all taxi drivers – he regaled us with the benefit of his experience as a father of four. Amongst his not-so-tactful gems was when he said that the first child should be kept until he or she was twelve, and then shot – his philosophy being that the first one would never be worth the trouble that he or she had caused.

I am happy to say that that was never the case with Wendy, although she has been married with a family of her own for many years now. Of course there were times that we worried about her, as all first time parents do; but she has never ceased to be a joy and pleasure to us. Not only do we love her as a daughter but we are also great friends too. As we grow older her devotion to us seems to increase every year.

Apart from Joan having an obscure illness just after Wendy was born, life settled down for the rest of the year as we got to grips with the mysteries of parenthood. Sometime in the spring we moved out of Joan's home into a place of our own. There was still a major housing shortage but we managed to get the tenancy of a council flat. Although this wasn't as grand as it sounds, being part of a converted Land Army hostel, it was palatial to us: hot and cold water, a proper bathroom, plus some new furniture – we wouldn't have changed places with anyone.

This sadly was not to last, the second half of the year being in complete contrast to the first. It was February when Joan found she was pregnant again. This didn't worry us, and at first all went well. Later, however, Joan began to have some doubts and in late August she went into premature labour and was rushed into Hereford Hospital where, on 22 August, our son Stephen was born.

Looking back over all the years of our marriage I can still say that the weeks that followed his birth were, without doubt, the worst of our married life. This time round there was none of the joy of the previous year when Wendy was born. Being some weeks premature, Stephen was very small and very ill and within minutes of being born was baptised by a Roman Catholic nurse. Sadly, despite an incubator being rushed some eighty miles, all the efforts of the nursing staff were to no avail. After a brief thirty hours in this world he passed from us. The child that neither of us had held, and I don't think Joan had even seen, had died. Over the years we have often wondered what he would have done; this year was a poignant birthday memory, as it would have been his fiftieth birthday.

While Joan lay in hospital recovering, I had to set about the business of arranging the burial and all the legal formalities that a birth and funeral requires. Bill came with me as we trudged around Hereford to find an undertaker and make all the arrangements. Joan was still in hospital when Stephen was laid to rest under the wall of Belmont Abbey. Many criticisms are made of the Catholic Church; I can only say that no one could have been more kind or helpful than the priests of Belmont Abbey were to me then and to Joan in the succeeding months. On one occasion a priest made a round trip of forty miles, in the rain, to visit us at Cross Ash.

Bill was the only support I had at the funeral; Sid tried to get there but got lost on the way. He did, however, get to Cross Ash to support me afterwards. This time there was no triumphal homecoming for Joan. Having Wendy to care for helped us over this sad period as we slowly put our lives back together.

In October I decided for a number of reasons that the dairy business wasn't working out as I had hoped, so I sold the business to go back into electrical contracting. This marked the end of my association with Monmouth. From now on I would only occasionally visit the town that had played such a major part in my life.

I worked for three or four small firms for the rest of the fifties. There was no such thing as work contracts then; you had a job as long as the employer had work, and at the end of the contract, or if work got short, it was a case of two hours' notice on Friday afternoons and off you went. One factor all these people had in common was a total disregard of their workers' safety. Ladders and steps were often of poor quality or unsuitable for the particular purpose. How there were not more accidents I do not know. Transport was also bad; men were expected to sit on cable drums, or their toolboxes, in the back of unsafe vans, while the employer drove furiously to or from the site in order to save time.

Another terrible thing then was the lack of proper toilet or catering facilities on building sites. At one site I worked on in Brecon, the toilets consisted of a rail over a large pit in the corner of a field. Woe betide anyone who overbalanced! Falling in would have been quite an easy thing to do. Catering was also primitive. Sometimes the builders would make a fire of scrap wood, and many times I have eaten my lunch while walking about to keep warm. Believe me, if there is anything colder than a building site in Brecon I have yet to find it. I am no lover of Labour governments, but the 1974 Health and Safety Act was a fine piece of legislation, overzealously enforced at times, but a good and long overdue act.

Apart from work, what of our personal life? 1954 saw us picking up the pieces and making steady progress. Later, Joan was pregnant again but thankfully appeared in good health this time. From October/November she had to visit Hereford Hospital every week; the doctors were making sure there were to be no mistakes this time. I was working for a character called Bill Lewis, who modestly described himself as an electrical, mechanical and refrigeration engineer. His business was in Abergavenny.

I was travelling home one Saturday afternoon in early December when just as I was approaching Cross Ash, a car coming towards me lost control on the corner and knocked me clean off my motorbike, I got up OK, went to move and fell over again – I had broken my ankle! I can't remember the sequence of events after; suffice to say that at five o'clock I was back in Hereford Hospital, this time as a patient. After the x-rays confirmed that I had a broken ankle, they decided that the joint needed plastering. As it was Saturday evening, there was only a small staff on duty, and my state of mind was not helped when I heard the duty doctor admitting to the nurse that he had never done any plastering before, I sincerely hope that he never did any again.

That night was one of the worst I have ever suffered. As the bruise came out, my ankle, encased in a tight plaster, started to swell. All night long I experienced severe pain, and next day had to return to the hospital to have it replastered. I can still recall the technician's face when, in reply to his shocked question, 'Wherever did you have this done?' I replied, 'Here!' However, after this, all went well and two weeks after Christmas I returned to work. Fair play to my employer, he kept my job for me, and I was able to start earning again.

We had a very quiet Christmas that year, but somehow we got through it. I was receiving the princely sum of three pounds fifteen shillings (£3.75) sickness benefit. Of this, sixteen shillings went to pay the rent, and Joan needed a pound for her weekly trip to Hereford, which left us about two pounds to live on. But live on it we did and manage to buy presents for Wendy. Joan was out one evening when I decided to sort out some pay packets, and lo and behold, I found a pound note in one of them, so Joan had a Christmas present also.

That winter of 1956 was the coldest for many years, with a lot of snow and ice. My motorbike was still at the repairer's, so I had to travel to work by bus. On the evening of 23 February I had managed to buy a sack of wood, which I took home on the bus.

That evening we burnt our last lump of coal. About two in the morning of the 24th Joan woke me up to say that she thought things might soon be happening. She has never forgiven me for telling her to hang on, as I didn't want to go out in the snow. At four o'clock, Joan knew the birth was definitely happening, so I had no option but to go out and get the ambulance. After twenty miles of sliding and slipping, the ambulance finally made it, although Joan did wonder if the baby would arrive before they got to the hospital. This time there were no complications; at about nine o'clock that morning Tony arrived in this world, the fine healthy boy we had hoped for.

Meanwhile, what was happening back at the ranch? After seeing Joan off, in order to conserve what wood I had, I waited as long as possible before getting Wendy up, and managed to keep her warm. Later in the day, as I sat by our last log, a guardian angel arrived in the unlikely guise of a coal-begrimed Mr Hancocks, our local coal merchant. He had a ton of coal for my father-in-law, but because of the snow was unable to deliver it, so he told him to bring it to me. Not only was I able to keep us warm, I was able to blackmail my neighbours into babysitting when I visited Joan or went to work.

Visiting Joan was a major problem. My motorbike was still under repair, there was no direct bus service and the roads were still very bad; salting the roads was still a thing of the future. The day was saved by our neighbour, Douggie. He took me as far as he could on his motorbike to a place where I was able to catch the bus. I was never able to have the full time with Joan, but it was well worth the effort. How different was Joan's homecoming this time! All the snow and ice had melted; the sun was shining on a beautiful spring day. Once again I had Alban Martin to bring them home, but this time he refrained from giving us any advice. Obviously he considered we had served our apprenticeship in child rearing.

A few weeks after they came home, my employer ran out of work, so being last in I was first out. There was no problem, as I got a job with a firm in Crickhowell. Having left one beautiful valley I found myself in another, the Usk, described by Isaak Walton as 'the heavenly incomparable'.

The firm in Crickhowell was run by two partners; both of them were good craftsmen, but having trained pre-war were way out of date, the one called Bill hopelessly so. He was a shortish, thickset man and, as befitted a Northerner, very canny about money. Travelling to a job with him was a hair-raising affair, as this was non-productive time; driving back was an even more hairy journey, as this was overtime. He was so mean that once after a dance he found someone had stolen his car, and after contacting the police, he turned to his wife with the words, 'Coom on, Bess, we'll have to walk.' And walk she had to – all six miles of it – because he was too mean to get a taxi.

If opposites make for a good partnership, this one should have been near perfect, the other member of the duo – Harold – was a tall, rather thin man. When Bill was building his bungalow Harold was helping him to fasten the ceiling board. To do this they slung a thin plank between two paint drums. Realising he didn't have a hammer Bill jumped off the plank, projecting his partner upwards into the ceiling... Harold's comments are not recorded.

To be fair, they had a good spread of work: rural electrification, new housing sites (at last the country was starting to move) and military work. The morning I started working for them was bleak and cold; the first job was re-wiring Brecon Barracks. This was 1956. The Suez Crisis had just been resolved and National Service had been resumed. One of my workmates, Glyn, had recently completed his apprenticeship and was awaiting his call up. I can still see his face as he gazed out of a window watching the recruits being drilled on that windswept square and his muttered comment, 'It's like watching you're own bloody funeral!'

As my job settled down, life at home moved on. Tony grew by leaps and bounds. Always a happy child, he was never a problem except when he and Wendy went down with whooping cough; for some time Joan and I never had a full night's sleep, until we had to recourse to one sleeping, and one nursing the children. Tough, yes, but worth it; we never regretted having any of our children, which was just as well, as Michael was on the way.

Michael was the only one of our children to be born at home and the only one where I was present at the birth. What a wonderful experience that was! The nurse who attended Joan was a Scots lady with a lovely sense of humour. After the birth, and after she had fixed up Joan, she turned to me with the words, 'Right, Dad, time for fags all round.' So we all relaxed in a cloud of smoke: just imagine that today!

I had arranged to take my fortnight's holiday to look after Joan and the children. When the nurse arrived the next morning, it was to find me with my feet up having a smoke. She was most put out, as she had spent the night worrying how I was going to cope – only to find Joan, Tony and Michael fed and asleep and Wendy out playing.

Having a family of this size and travelling some thirty miles a day to work made us realise that we would need a bigger house, preferably nearer my work. We looked at various places and eventually we settled on a cottage on the Llangattock Mountain some two miles from Crickhowell.

Wyeswood – the Final Chapter

A year after Ted and Ina were married, Ted was posted to the Suez Canal area, and as they had no home Ina came to stay with us at Wyeswood. This was never a happy arrangement, as Ina never really adapted to life in the country. Although everybody tried their best, I think it was with relief all round when she was finally allowed to join him. I think that they had about twelve months in Egypt living in a rented flat before things went all wrong for them. They had just started on a fortnight's leave when the Egyptians rebelled against their king, the whole country was in turmoil and they had to return to the base at Alexandria for their own safety. Ted was given an armed guard to recover some of their possessions from the flat; he refused to make another trip as he felt that it would put the men at too great a risk.

Because the whole of the Canal Zone was now an active service area, all women and children were repatriated to the UK. I don't think Ina stayed long at Wyeswood but she was certainly there for our wedding; Ted returned to the UK sometime in 1953.

Looking back now I realise that that year (1953) was quite a momentous year for my parents. In March the first grandchild (Jackie) arrived on the scene. In August, Wendy was born, but the greatest shock of all was when, early in the year, Bill decided to get married. Bill had given up the dairy farming the previous year to start pig farming at Wyeswood. To pay his way he went to work for Frank's firm as a builder's labourer, but at the time that Joan and I got married there was no hint that there was a romance in the air.

The shock was not that he was getting married, but who he was marrying. Bill had never been short of girlfriends, but when he told us that he was marrying our cousin, Freda, everyone was taken by surprise. Freda had had the misfortune to be born with only half her right arm. This was regarded by many as a sort of stigma on the family; it took six hours for the midwife to summon up the courage to tell Freda's mother the news.

Living with such a disability must have been hard; living with other people's attitude to such a disability must have been even harder. Many people would associate this handicap with a mental deficiency. Typical of this attitude was the way people would address questions about her to her mother, as if she was incapable of answering for herself.

This attitude must have been particularly hard for Freda, as she does possess a good brain and doubtless, had she had today's opportunities, would have gone to university. Despite all this, she got a job with Woolworth's, no mean feat in the conditions that prevailed before the war. She was still working for them (as a supervisor) up to the time of her marriage.

The wedding took place on a lovely Spring day in May 1953, in Freda's home town of Caerphilly, where I returned the compliment of being his best man, as he had for me a few months before.

If that year was eventful for my parents, the next year was hardly less so. In April, Ina, Ted's wife, gave birth to Claire, and Sid gave up working in London and got a job in Newport. To provide somewhere to live he bought a caravan which he parked at Wyeswood. Later he bought a plot of land and built a house in Newport.

Sometime early that year my father decided to retire. He sold everything he had relating to poultry farming, all the buildings and equipment that had been so painfully acquired over the years were sold. His last horse and the trap, which had been such a part of his life, went to Uncle Sid. The rest of his time at Wyeswood he confined himself to keeping sheep. That year, when Claire was christened, was to be the last occasion that we would ever be together as a family. It was also the last time that Ina was at Wyeswood; for some strange reason she had taken a strong dislike to my parents, especially Dad. Why I shall never know; he had done everything he could to make her comfortable when she stayed with us, but it was obviously not appreciated.

The year of 1955 and the early part 1956 were fairly quiet for my parents but the clouds were gathering again. Sometime in that year my mother developed a tremor in her hands, and hospital tests revealed that she had Parkinson's disease. From then on their lives went steadily downhill as my mother's condition worsened. Instead of enjoying the happy retirement they so richly deserved, they had to cope with that terrible affliction.

Life was made easier for them in 1955 when at long last they were connected to the electricity supply. My father had tried various generators over the years but none was really successful; once connected they lost no time in getting all the appliances they could, including television, a far cry from that first radio set that he bought in 1937. Although they were not able to enjoy it for long, I like to think that at least it gave them some comfort in those last, troubled years.

It was a lovely October day in 1958 when I saw my mother for the last time. Bill had sent me a message to say that Mum was declining fast. Although she was by then almost completely paralysed, her mind was still sharp and clear; only the previous day she had been reading the daily paper.

The following day Bill came to fetch all of us, but sadly we were too late to be with her when she finally passed away. My father was, of course, devastated. Theirs had been a love story that had lasted for nearly fifty years; during all that time they only lived for each other and for us. I often think that I alone of the family knew how deep that devotion was, having been with them during the terrible years of war, especially with Stan's death and all the upheavals of moving, as Dad tried everything he could to ameliorate her suffering. When she died, he also died in spirit. Only with Joan and me would he ever experience a real settled home again.

It was lovely warm autumn that year, and it was a lovely sunny day, the day we laid her to rest in Trelech churchyard, the plot being virtually given to my father in recognition of his many years of support to the church.

As Joan and I walked up the path towards the family home, we realised we would never see her face at the kitchen window again, as she waited to welcome us in once more. A life that had started in that now faraway time and place in Fulham, a life that had been always devoted to the welfare of others, was now over. As we grieved there was one corner of our hearts that was glad that her sufferings were over. Uncle Bert gave a poignant sidelight on her earlier life, when he remarked that when he was young Vi (my mum) 'was someone who came home once a year'. A grim reminder of what life 'in service' was like for young girls in the early part of the twentieth century.

After the funeral I went back to work, believing that with both Sid and Bill living so close Dad would be looked after. Sid had at last got his house habitable and moved to Newport, and Bill was busy with his business. Just after Christmas I went to visit my father, only to find that he was lodging with a woman who didn't really want him. It was heartbreaking to see what was left of his furniture stacked outside covered by a sheet.

Obviously something had to be done, and after various twists and turns he finally came to us at Dan-y-Coed. This all happened very suddenly, before we had time to make any arrangements to accommodate him. We only had two bedrooms then, so for six weeks Joan and I had to sleep on the sofa until I could arrange for some of his furniture to come to us and the rest to go into store.

To say that the next eight months were hard going is really understating the situation. It wasn't that we resented having him but it was especially hard for Joan. Wendy had started school the year before. As we were just under two miles from the school, transport was not available, so Joan had to take Wendy to school and collect her in the afternoons. This was in addition to all the housework and cooking for six of us. This was not helped by my father's state of mind; having to answer the same question several times a day is tough going, and by the end of the summer Joan was down to about six stones.

This obviously was not a situation that could last. Ted was due to come home in August (he had been in Singapore for some years) and we all (especially Dad) hoped that he could help us resolve the situation. He, Ina and Claire duly came to stay with us in August, giving Joan three more to look after. The only thing Ted did was to make a few stupid suggestions – all avoiding any effort his part, of course. After persuading my father to change his will in his favour, they left two weeks later, never to make any contact with us ever again.

A month later my father, realising that Ted was not going to be any use, asked me to arrange for him to go into a retirement home. This was not the way we had envisaged him spending his last days, but for Joan's and the children's sake I had no option but to do just that.

Dad was only ten days in the retirement home before he suffered a major stroke and was moved to St David's Hospital in Brecon. He never recovered from the stroke, and therefore this was to be his last 'home'.

A bitterly cold easterly wind swept across Trelech churchyard as we laid him to rest, beside his beloved Vi, on a January day in 1962. On that day a chapter closed, our lives would never be the same again. From now on we would be not one family but four, and never again would our destinies cross.

Epilogue: Sixty Years Later

'It's somewhere here,' said Audrey as we travelled down the Wye Valley Road. 'It' was a guest house, 'somewhere between Llandogo and Trelech'. This puzzled me somewhat as I could not remember a farm anywhere between those villages, and as Audrey was not sure of the directions it was all a bit of a mystery. The mystery was resolved when I realised, to my great delight, that the 'Old Farmhouse', where we were to stay for three nights, was indeed what had been the home of my father's friend, Bill Morgan.

How come we were in the Wye Valley, you ask. As it happened we were in Britain on our way back to Spain after going to Australia for our granddaughter's wedding. I had long wanted to show Joan more of the place where I grew up. Mike and Audrey wanted to see it as well, so it seemed an ideal time to do it.

I must admit that I had a few doubts about returning to the area after so long an interval. Changes I knew there would be, but what they might be I could not guess. The first changes were obvious as soon as we got out the car. The house obviously had had to be altered to suit its new role; the cider house, which was the first place where I had ever seen cider produced, and was a bike shelter for us if we were catching the bus, had gone to make way for housing, but no one could criticise the way it had been done.

Mid-afternoon, and having settled I was anxious to start showing them Llandogo, so uphill we went, past the old doctor's surgery (now a private house) to the bottom of the Cleddon waterfalls. A big improvement here, as a path has been made from top to bottom. We walked a fair part, but the path being wet we decided to abandon the walk. Luckily, the sun still shone, so they saw it at its best.

Everyone was ready to keep walking so I took them through the woods up the Trelech road. Here there was little change over the years except for a few extra footpaths and more deciduous trees.

Into my heart from an air that kills
From yon far country blows
What are those blue remembered hills?
What spires? What farms are these?

That is the land of lost content
I see it shining plain
The happy highways where I went
And cannot come again

—from *A Shropshire Lad*
by A E Housman

Fifty-two and a half years later: Joan and myself outside the church where we were married.

Entrance to Wyeswood, the scene of many sad partings.

Myself outside Whitelye Farm with Harold Johns, the present owner, 2005.

Catbrook Church, where I reluctantly spent many a Sunday afternoon.

Appendix: *My Parents*

My grandparents' home where my mother was born
Image from Fulham Public Library

My mother was born at No. 47 (25 November 1888). If the photo (top) of the dairy is No. 1, then her home would be at the far end of the street. The dairy in the lower photo is probably the one

107

where her brother Will worked before the war. He was later killed on the Somme.

Lower Town Farm, Preston Wynne, Herefordshire. What a contrast with my mother's birthplace. Photograph by Tony Powell.

This was where my father was born (23 January 1888). What a contrast to Dieppe Street! Who would have thought that two people from such different backgrounds would ever meet? But meet they did, and had as long and as happy a marriage as was possible for such a star-crossed generation.

Where I was born. Photograph by Ray Powell

Wyeswood was about 300 yards from this signpost, always a very welcome sight. The place names on the stone milepost were chiselled out in 1940 in case of invasion.

Map of Catbrook

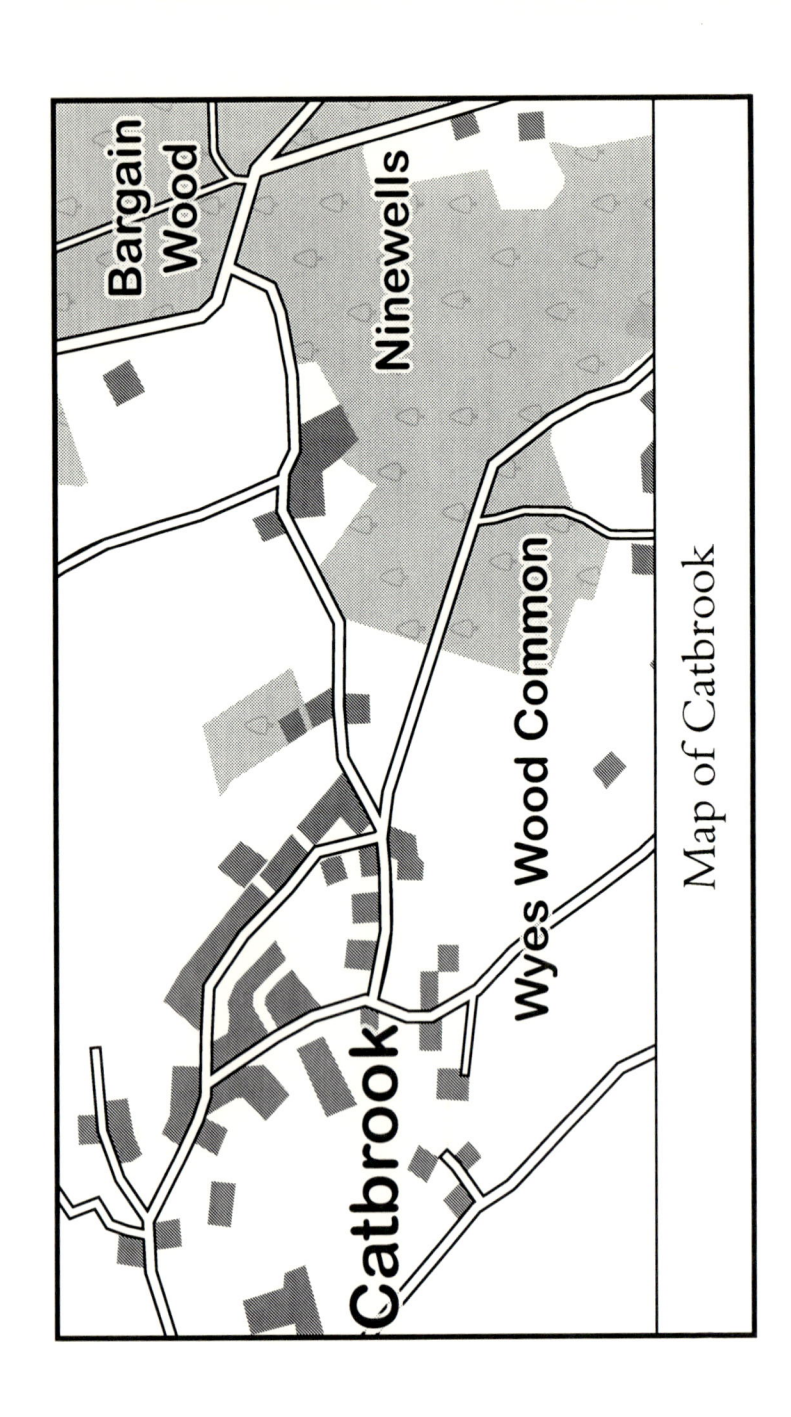

Wedding day, 1916

I believe that this is a photo taken on my parents' wedding day in April 1916. She is proudly showing her wedding ring. To my knowledge she never removed it, and at her request it was buried with her.

She was almost the eldest of thirteen children born to my grandparents, eleven of them surviving infancy.

Her father, who rejoiced in the name of William Larkin Thompson, was born near Deal in Kent. He was a time-served carpenter; where he served his apprenticeship is not known, or why he moved to London, where I presume he met my grandmother. Unfortunately he lost an arm repairing a sash window but still managed to maintain his family, though this must have been hard, especially for my grandmother. Precise records are scarce, but I do know that between 1910 and 1916 she lost four children, and her husband in 1914.

My mum never spoke a lot of her teenage years, or what was happening with her family. To us, looking back in time at those years, it seems rather strange that there was such a gulf between the elder and younger siblings; because the families were large, the elder ones had to leave home to make way for the younger ones. My father often spoke of his mother having two families, or has he put it, 'the first and second hatch'. For instance by the time my Uncle Sid was born his elder brother was serving in the Boer War.

Mum, being one of the older ones, spent her teens and most of her twenties 'in service', a hard and gruelling life of long hours at the beck and call of everyone. By the 1908 she had established herself as the cook, which gave her a better job and higher wages; despite all this she regularly sent money home to help her mother support the family.

Wedding day, 1916

As far as I know, this photo of my father was taken on their wedding day. He was the sixth child of a family of twelve, all of whom survived childhood. His father came from a long line of Herefordshire farmers. At the time of my father's birth he was farming at Preston Wynne. The 1890s were not a good time for farming, and my grandfather had to move shortly after my father was born. At the time of the 1901 census he was employed as a farm bailiff. This decline in my grandfather's fortunes meant, perforce, that my father had to find work in the only thing he knew anything about – farming.

His first job, on a fairly large farm, was to help to look after six pairs of shire horses, which were used for the work around the farm. His first task in the morning was to fill the leather cider bottles for the horsemen who had to start work at six o'clock in the morning. Each man was entitled to two quart bottles which he took with him to the fields. At ten o'clock it was my father's job to go around the farm replenishing the bottles, I presume that they went home at midday for 'dinner', this being the time for the main meal of the day. I don't know if all the men drunk their full allowance but my father told me of one man who was so drunk that he had to crawl to the side of the field to drink even more; and then crawl back – to sit on a mowing machine, of all things! The day finished at six when he had to help feed the horses.

A succession of farm jobs followed including time in a hop yard, until fate took him to work for Lord Davies, near Newport. Lord Davies was the man who built Barry docks. At the public inquiry which preceded the building, the opposing QC remarked snootily, 'You started your working life as a sawyer, I believe?' To which the then Mr Davies replied, 'Yes, and if I only had your brains I'd be a sawyer today.

Thirty years later, April 1946. The line in the middle is where I cut the photo in half so I could keep it with me when I was living in Iodoinos.

Which of them arrived at Newport first I do not know, it was sometime around 1910 when they first met. It was a long-range courtship, as father went to work in Nantwich, Cheshire in 1912. I think the outbreak of the First World War delayed their plans somewhat; he volunteered for the army before they married, as he did not want to make a widow of my mother – a likely possibility, given the high casualty rate at the time. However his health was so bad (he was crippled with rheumatism) that the army, desperate as they were for recruits, turned him down.

That first year in Nantwich would have been wonderful for them had it not been for the war. For the first time they had a home of their own, but the happiness was soured by tragedy. In the September of the previous year, Dad's brother Jim was killed at the Battle of Loos; just three months after the wedding, Mum's favourite brother, Will, was killed on the second day of the Battle of the Somme.

Mum had always looked forward to having a family of her own, so the sadness of loss must have been helped when she became pregnant with my sister, Stella; but even this joy was not to be, as my sister was stillborn; my father buried her in Nantwich churchyard. Two of his workmates carried the tiny white coffin. This was to be the only girl my mother would ever have.

Taken a few months before the death of Ernest.

The year of 1918 brought peace and Mum's first boy, my brother Ernest, the taller of the two in the photo. Sid, the one on the chair, arrived in 1920. Shortly after this they moved to Llancarfan, near Barry, where the rest of us were born.

My father had a good job there, and they should have been set for a happy period, but again they were to be disappointed. In 1921 Ernest became ill – with what, my parents never knew. All Mum ever said was, 'He just faded away.' He died later that year, and lies now in the churchyard of Llancarfan, the church where the rest of us would be christened.

These then were my parents. Like all of us they were the products of their age. Born when the motor car had only just been invented – by the time of my father's death man was already in space. Their generation lived through the two most horrific wars in history. Looking around at what this generation enjoys today, I can only think what an immense debt we owe to that generation. I just hope that future generations will appreciate their sacrifices and cherish their inheritance.

The first photo of the whole family.
Back row: Sid and Stan. Front: Myself, Bill, Ted.
It also shows the construction of the house, c. 1931.

The only photo ever taken of the whole family. It was taken in front of the kitchen that Dad built in 1946. To the left is the Bargain Wood.
Left to right: Sid, Bill, myself and Ted, c. 1954.

Stan, ten days before his death in November 1942.

*Barry Island, 1952.
Not a Sunday School trip!*

Stan and Bill, given our family musical talents, the most unlikely choirboys ever!

My father with the trophies he won the year he swept the board at the MIA trials.
My faithful dog, Joe, in the background.

To be a farmer's boy! Myself with Flower, 1943.

From left to right: Joan and Wendy, Dad, Ina and Claire, Mum, Vera and Jackie.

My future bride – Joan, June 1952

My lovely wife and me at our wedding.

*Too late now!
Bridesmaids: Edie and Mary.*

Printed in the United Kingdom
by Lightning Source UK Ltd.
124580UK00001B/14/A